The
Data Teams
Experience

A GUIDE FOR
Effective Meetings

Angela Peery

**LEAD+
LEARN
PRESS**

ENGLEWOOD, COLORADO

The Leadership and Learning Center
317 Inverness Way South, Suite 150
Englewood, Colorado 80112
Phone 1.866.399.6019 | Fax 303.504.9417
www.LeadandLearn.com

Published by Lead + Learn Press, a division of Advanced Learning Centers, Inc.

Library of Congress Cataloging-in-Publication Data

Peery, Angela B., 1964-
 The data teams experience : a guide for effective meetings / Angela Peery.
   p. cm.
 Includes index.
  ISBN 978-1-935588-02-3 (alk. paper)
 1. Educational evaluation. 2. Teachers—Professional relationships. 3. Teacher effectiveness. 4. Meetings—Planning. I. Title.
   LB2822.75.P44 2011
   371.102—dc22
                                                      2011007933

ISBN 978-1-935588-02-3

Printed in the United States of America

15 14 13 12 11   03 04 05 06 07

The
Data Teams
Experience

Contents

About the Author

Angela Peery, Ed.D.

Dr. Angela Peery is a Senior Professional Development Associate at The Leadership and Learning Center and is a teacher, researcher, and writer. Just before joining The Center, she worked for the South Carolina Department of Education as an instructional coach at a low-achieving middle school. Previously, she was also a literacy consultant for the National Urban Alliance for Effective Education, working with teachers in high-poverty schools in Seattle and Indianapolis.

Dr. Peery's experience includes ten years of classroom teaching at the secondary level, four years as a high school assistant principal, and various curriculum leadership roles at the building, district, and state levels. She has taught graduate education courses at Coastal Carolina University and the University of Phoenix Online and is a codirector of a National Writing Project site. She has also taught undergraduate composition for Horry-Georgetown Technical College and Kaplan University Online.

In 2000, Dr. Peery earned her doctorate in curriculum and instruction. During her dissertation research phase of almost two years, she worked with a Jewish day school to improve literacy instruction. She is the author of five books and also has created seminars and training manuals for The Center.

Dr. Peery is a native of Salem, Virginia, and holds degrees from Randolph–Macon Woman's College, Hollins College, and the University of South Carolina. Her professional licensures include secondary English, secondary administration, and gifted/talented education.

Her family consists of husband Tim, three Labrador retrievers, and a cat. They reside on Lady's Island in the Beaufort/Hilton Head area of South Carolina. Angela is an officer in her homeowners' association. In her spare time, she enjoys leisure travel and boating.

Dr. Peery can be reached at APeery@LeadandLearn.com.

Acknowledgments

Having been a Data Team member myself, I can attest to the hard work that goes into making the entire Data Teams process work well for both teachers and students.

Writing a book about Data Team meetings has been both exhausting and joyous. I strived to capture the work of dozens of teams with whom I've consulted in addition to the fine work of many colleagues at The Leadership and Learning Center. The only thing I'm sure of is that I have not adequately represented the expertise and dedication that all these educators exhibit.

First, I must thank my own Data Team leader, Angela Binkley, for the meetings she orchestrated in the 2002/03 school year at Whale Branch Middle School in Beaufort, South Carolina. She taught us all much about patience, perseverance, and focus, plus she always displayed grace in dealing with our various passions and prejudices. The ripple effects of her inspired leadership continue to this day.

My Center colleagues Lisa Almeida, Laura Besser, Juan Cordova, Tony Flach, Tracey Flach, Linda Gregg, and Ray Smith have shared their abundant Data Teams knowledge and experience with me freely, and for that I'm grateful. Readers will benefit from their contributions, which lie behind every word in this book.

My colleagues Kristin Anderson, Lauren Campsen, Kris Nielsen, Barb Pitchford, Jay Trujillo, and John Van Pelt are sincerely thanked for the views on Data Teams that they shared with me and others, both in published and unpublished forms, and through personal conversation and correspondence.

Colleague and former superintendent Steve Ventura and principals Jenny Delmarter and Loreda Clevenger (Edison School District, California) advanced my personal research on Data Teams immeasurably in the 2009/10 school year, and thus I'm indebted to them as well.

Administrators and teachers in Elkhart Community Schools (Indiana) have implemented and refined Data Teams over the past few years, and I've been fortunate enough to be a part of their journey. Particular thanks go to Chris Baldridge, Dave Benak, Leanne Geary, John Hill, Melissa Jennette, Jeff Komins, Jennie Mast, Dave McGuire, Richie Mendez, Josh Nice, Brad Sheppard, and Martha Strickler for always sharing their ideas openly and honestly in order to advance my own thinking—and for their tireless commitment to students.

Katie Schellhorn has been a supportive collaborator in this endeavor and makes all publishing with Lead + Learn Press a delight.

Last, the founder of The Leadership and Learning Center, Doug Reeves, has made the work that my colleagues and I do on behalf of Data Teams possible. Thank you, Doug, for allowing all of us to impact the daily lives of thousands of students. You always help us remember that our work matters.

CHAPTER 1

Data Teams and Alphabet Soup

> *Data Teams adhere to continuous improvement cycles, examine patterns and trends, and establish specific timelines, roles, and responsibilities to facilitate analysis that results in action.*
>
> —WHITE, 2005

Data Teams is a term created by The Leadership and Learning Center to describe how data-driven decision making is conducted at the classroom practitioner level. Data Teams follow a specific, proven process to examine student work, apply instructional strategies, and monitor student learning in response to the enacted strategies.

DT, PLC, NCLB, RTI—the abundant acronyms can sometimes seem like a bowl of alphabet soup. The intent of this chapter, in question-and-answer format, is to provide clarity about what Data Teams are and what they do, in addition to explaining how they are related to other current topics and concepts in educational improvement.

What Are Instructional Data Teams?

So many acronyms and jargon-y terms exist in education. *Data Teams* may seem like another in a long list of such gimmicky names. However, if understood fully, it is a term that signifies true professional collaboration among educators and high achievement among students.

An instructional Data Team is a small grade-level, department, course-alike, or organizational team that examines work generated from a common formative assessment.

Let's examine that definition more closely, *starting with the composition of the team.*

A Data Team may consist of an entire grade level, and often does, especially in an elementary school. So a K–5 school might have one Data Team at each level: a kindergarten team, a first-grade team, a second-grade team, and so on. In large elementary schools, in rare instances, multiple teams may exist at each grade level if having separate teams makes frequent meetings more manageable. So, for example, if there are eight fourth-grade teachers in one school, there may be a Data Team 4A and a Data Team 4B, each consisting of four teachers. Center associates have worked with many highly effective large Data Teams, however, and recommend that if at all possible, an entire grade level team remain intact.

In some cases, elementary Data Teams are departmentalized. For example, in some K–5 schools, fifth-grade students have their mathematics instruction with one teacher, language arts with another, and science with yet another. Some Data Teams address this situation by focusing on interdisciplinary skills, like nonfiction writing or problem solving. If there are two fifth-grade teams in such an instance, the two teachers of each subject could also form a small Data Team (the fifth-grade language arts team, and so on).

At the middle and high school levels, department and course-alike teams are common. So a middle school might have an English language arts Data Team that covers grades 6 through 8, with two teachers at each grade level, making a total of six teachers on this vertical team. In that same middle school, another possible configuration would be to have teams of two English language arts teachers at each grade level. Because a team of two is so small, other educators, like ELL specialists, special education teachers, instructional coaches, and elective-course teachers, are often included so that each team consists of three members or more.

In high schools, the most obvious configuration for a Data Team is a group of teachers who teach the same course. Another possible configuration is across disciplines by special interest. One example of this type of team would be in an academy setting in which math, English, science, history, and specialized electives teachers group together and share students across the team.

In both middle and high schools, there are often teachers of "singleton" courses—meaning that a particular course is taught by only one person. Various ways to handle this situation are discussed in Chapter 8.

Let's unpack the rest of the definition of Data Teams: *They examine work generated from common formative assessments.*

Common formative assessments (CFAs) are assessments given by all the teachers on a Data Team to all of the students they share. These assessments are ideally selected or created by the team members. The items on a common formative assessment focus squarely on prioritized standards and/or learning goals and are carefully aligned with national, provincial, state, and system tests (Leadership and Learning Center, 2006a).

It is the student work on CFAs that is analyzed in meetings and that serves as the basis for the discussion of changes in instructional practice. Because the main goal of the assessments is for teachers to ascertain the current picture of student learning and adjust their actions accordingly, these assessments are generally not used to determine students' grades.

What Do These Teams Do?

Data Teams hold collaborative, structured, scheduled meetings that focus on the effectiveness of teaching and learning. Issues not directly related to student learning or instructional practice are tabled and discussed at other times.

The Data Teams process includes six explicit steps, five of which are followed in every meeting at which assessment data is analyzed (Leadership and Learning Center, 2010, p. 9). Briefly, the five basic meeting steps are as follows. These steps are discussed in great detail in Chapter 7.

1. **Collect and chart/display the data.**

2. **Analyze data and prioritize needs.** Analyze student performance based on CFAs to determine the strengths and challenges that students are demonstrating. Prioritize the student learning needs that will be addressed by the changes in instructional practice.

3. **Set, review, and revise incremental SMART goals.** (These are goals that are specific, measurable, achievable, relevant, and timely.)

4. **Select common instructional strategies to be employed to address the learning challenges discovered in Step Two.** The team may consider both strategies to be implemented in large-group or whole-class instruction and those to be implemented with differentiated performance groups.

5. **Determine results indicators.** Results indicators complete the statement: "When this strategy is implemented, we expect to see the following evidence of its effectiveness." Results indicators thus serve as a monitoring tool for the team (Leadership and Learning Center, 2010, p. 124). Results indicators delineate both what adults do and how students perform.

The Center recommends that teams use this five-step process at least once a month. Many of the most successful teams that Center associates have worked with follow the five-step process twice a month or more frequently (Leadership and Learning Center, 2006b, p. 72).

When new assessment information is not available, Data Teams may hold monitoring meetings to discuss how the selected instructional strategies are working, to adjust instructional strategies, to check their pacing with each other, to plan lessons, or to examine additional work samples. Data Teams operate in a continuous improvement process, so even when there is not "fresh" student achievement data to examine, they engage in monitoring their use of strategies and how those strategies are impacting students.

Additional meetings of the team include those meetings at which common formative assessments are designed and/or revised or at which curriculum maps are created or adjusted.

Some teams have used the time between common formative assessments to undertake specific professional development related to their collective inquiry. For example, a specific high school team may want to study effective note-taking methods because they determine that their students do not take notes that help them learn concepts deeply, and the incomplete understanding is evidenced in the assessment results.

Why Are Data Teams an Essential Part of a Data-Driven Decision-Making Process?

Data-driven decision making is a mindset. It is a continuous improvement cycle in which educators use data to improve teaching, learning, and leadership.

In a school, data-driven decision making includes the close examination of data so that the performance of various groups can be examined and so that a full picture of student achievement emerges. The practice also includes the setting of student achievement goals and determining what the adults in the building will do to work toward those goals. Both the number and frequency of Data Team meetings, in addition to other adult actions like the amount of time administrators and coaches observe instruction, are organizational strategies that often boost achievement.

Data Teams operate within this framework of continuous improvement to get at the heart of learning and to make immediate changes to instructional practice. Without teachers acting decisively and frequently on formative assessment information that is available to them, school achievement goals are often not met.

How are Data Teams Part of True Professional Learning Communities (PLCs), Resulting in Improved Instruction for All Students?

The publication of *Professional Learning Communities at Work: Best Practices for Enhancing Student Achievement* by DuFour and Eaker in 1998 ignited new interest in schools operating as true learning organizations. Richard and Rebecca DuFour and their colleagues have since published other books and numerous articles on the PLC concept.

According to this influential, original book, when a school is a true PLC, its members collectively pursue a shared mission and shared goals. They work interdependently in teams that are focused on student learning. They engage in collective inquiry into best practice. As a result of their inquiry, they innovate in order to continuously improve student achievement.

If Professional Learning Communities are the "what" of school improvement, then the practices of Data Teams serve as the "how." The five-step process that Data Teams use in their meetings, along with the added sixth step of monitoring the effectiveness of selected innovations, provides a flexible framework in which educators can realize what it means to operate as a learning community.

Many schools have tried to implement their versions of the PLC concept but have experienced limited success. Simply holding meetings called "PLCs" does not ensure that the teachers involved will use the time to directly impact student learning. In fact, simply holding such meetings doesn't guarantee that teachers *even know how to collaborate effectively!*

Many veteran teachers have spent much of their careers working in isolation, planning lessons, designing assessments, and reflecting on instruction as a team of only one. Thus, the specific Data Teams structures and processes help teachers navigate the unfamiliar territory of learning-focused collaboration. As the structures and processes are adapted over time to fit the unique needs of each team, student learning soars—and teacher learning does, too.

How Can Data Teams Help Schools Meet the Demands of No Child Left Behind and Other Mandates?

No Child Left Behind legislation (NCLB) brings statutory muscle to the general expectation that schools must serve all students. The goals of NCLB differ from the goals of earlier times, when some students were served well while others were not. Serving all students requires new ways of working as educators: collaboration has become a must, not an option. Schools must now operate as *learning* organizations, not just as *teaching* organizations. (See Exhibit 1.1 for more information about schools as learning organizations.)

When analyzing student work as part of the Data Teams process, teams determine which students are already proficient, which are close to being proficient, and which are

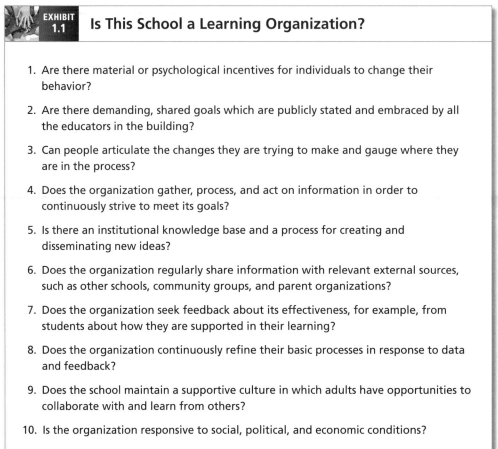

EXHIBIT 1.1   Is This School a Learning Organization?

1. Are there material or psychological incentives for individuals to change their behavior?

2. Are there demanding, shared goals which are publicly stated and embraced by all the educators in the building?

3. Can people articulate the changes they are trying to make and gauge where they are in the process?

4. Does the organization gather, process, and act on information in order to continuously strive to meet its goals?

5. Is there an institutional knowledge base and a process for creating and disseminating new ideas?

6. Does the organization regularly share information with relevant external sources, such as other schools, community groups, and parent organizations?

7. Does the organization seek feedback about its effectiveness, for example, from students about how they are supported in their learning?

8. Does the organization continuously refine their basic processes in response to data and feedback?

9. Does the school maintain a supportive culture in which adults have opportunities to collaborate with and learn from others?

10. Is the organization responsive to social, political, and economic conditions?

Source: Adapted from Brandt (2003)

further away. Sometimes teams design differentiated instruction for the various performance groups, employing a wide range of effective instructional strategies.

Students who remain nonproficient after multiple assessment cycles may be targeted for intensive assistance. It is often the performance of these very same students that has remained "hidden" and then later adversely affected a school's standardized test scores. By the time a school analyzes its year-end test score reports, it is too late—the students are gone for the summer, and children have slipped through the cracks. Data Teams monitor assessment data in a proactive, not reactive, manner. Schools that implement Data Teams are constantly monitoring information aligned with end-of-year achievement and thus prevent many of those same students from slipping through the cracks.

How Are Data Teams Related to RTI?

Response to Intervention (RTI) is a relatively new acronym in the professional educator's lexicon. RTI was formally authorized in December 2004 as part of the Individuals with Disabilities Education Act (IDEA) and has become a prominent component of the data-gathering and data-analysis processes of schools.

Basically, RTI is a process by which schools document a child's response to research-based interventions using a tiered approach of services. The interventions are designed to increase student learning in areas where the student appears to be struggling. The tiers represent increasingly intensive and personalized interventions.

At its core, RTI is about *good instruction.* Educators observe and document student learning, use specific methods to increase the learning of selected students, and evaluate the effectiveness of the methods used. As students work their way through the tiers of services, they receive increasingly intensive assistance designed to help them perform on grade level.

The six steps of the full Data Teams process in a school align very well with the federal requirements for RTI. There are only a few things educators should be mindful of in addition to the six-step process.

RTI requires "universal screening." Universal screening is initially undertaken early in the school year to determine which students may not meet grade-level standards and which students may have behavioral or emotional problems that interfere with learning. Follow-ups to this initial screening should be conducted at least two more times in the school year and can be a valuable part of the Data Teams process.

RTI also mandates a "problem-solving process" that investigates the strengths, challenges, and root causes of the learning problems of students who were identified in the universal screening. This process can be integrated with what is done at Step Two in any Data Team meeting and can also form the basis for other meetings focused solely on those students and their needs.

Tier One of RTI calls for high-quality, core instruction. This idea is fundamental to the entire Data Teams process. When teams meet and examine student work, the strategies they commit to employing should first be considered in the context of excellent, whole-class instruction. In other words, one of the first considerations at Step Four in the process should be the question, "Which instructional strategies can we use in core instruction to move the greatest number of students to proficiency?" The team should already have a good idea of the students who are closest to proficiency; those students have been considered in setting the SMART goal. But a secondary consideration should be, "How can we use the effective strategies we have agreed upon to impact the largest number of students possible?"

Tiers Two and Three are the levels of increasingly intensive services, meaning that the students get more help (more time, more frequently) and perhaps work with personnel other than the teacher who provides core instruction. After a complete Data Team cycle, in which a pre-assessment and post-assessment have been given, the students who remain nonproficient may be candidates for Tier Two intervention. This kind of targeted assistance is then carried out, monitored, and evaluated. If the student has still not made sufficient progress, he is now moved to the third tier, called "intensive intervention." All the while, excellent core instruction is still occurring for the entire range of students the particular Data Team serves, and the Data Teams process continues. Tier Two and Tier Three interventions do not supplant core instruction but work along with it. Likewise, RTI complements the Data Teams process—it does not supplant it.

Conclusion

Data Teams generate common formative assessments based on prioritized standards and then meet frequently to examine these assessments so that they can improve instruction. Instructional Data Teams are grade-level, department, course, or content-area teams that use a six-step process for results. The work of Data Teams exhibits the true qualities of Professional Learning Communities (PLCs) and also helps educators comply with the demands set forth in current legislation, including No Child Left Behind (NCLB) and Response to Intervention (RTI). When Data Teams are implemented effectively in a school, they are the vehicle that moves the school from a teaching organization to a learning organization.

CHAPTER 2

Getting Started—Focus, Structure, and Communication

Data Teams are the single best way to help educators ...
move from "drowning in data" to using information to
make better instructional decisions.

—REEVES, 2009

Schools use Data Teams to increase student achievement across grade levels and content areas. Data Teams are driven by their most burning questions about student learning. These questions lead them to discover their students' most urgent needs. Often, the teams begin with questions generated during a close examination of available data on student learning, which may be from state standardized tests or system benchmark assessments.

This chapter discusses how schools form Data Teams, how Data Teams begin the process of setting incremental achievement goals and using instructional strategies to reach those goals, and how the work of Data Teams is communicated both within the school and with stakeholders outside the school.

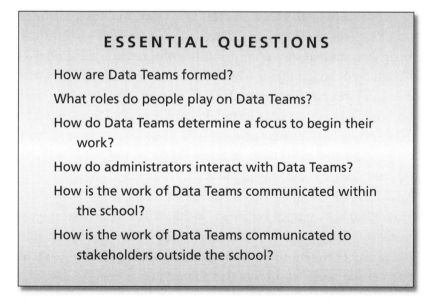

ESSENTIAL QUESTIONS

How are Data Teams formed?

What roles do people play on Data Teams?

How do Data Teams determine a focus to begin their work?

How do administrators interact with Data Teams?

How is the work of Data Teams communicated within the school?

How is the work of Data Teams communicated to stakeholders outside the school?

How Are Data Teams Formed?

Data Teams can be organized in a number of ways but are joined together through the use of a common formative assessment. Obviously, a team must consist of two or more people, but there is no "right" size for a Data Team.

A *horizontal* Data Team is one that covers an entire grade level. So at the elementary level, a second-grade team would ideally consist of all second-grade teachers in the school. Others may be part of this team as well. For example, if there is a special education teacher who serves many of the second-grade students, he would be a natural fit for the team. And, in elementary schools, physical education, music, and art teachers often serve as part of a specific grade-level team; these members are often able to add richness to the team's dialogue because of the different ways in which they interact with students.

At the middle school level, a horizontal team would consist of teachers of various subjects. Some of these teams can also be quite large. For example, an eighth-grade team I was once part of consisted of two English language arts teachers, two social studies teachers, two science teachers, two mathematics teachers, a special education co-teacher, and a teacher of modern dance. On an interdisciplinary team such as this one, the team must determine an area of focus that impacts all subject areas, like essay writing or drawing conclusions, and create assessment tasks accordingly.

In some cases, a horizontal team may consist of clusters of subject areas. For example, my own Data Team could have been configured with the science and math teachers as one team (four members) and the English language arts and social studies teachers as another (four members). The special education teacher could have been added to one group of four, and the dance teacher to the other, resulting in two teams of five members.

At the high school level, horizontal teams are rare, but are sometimes used in academy-type settings or for specialized needs. So an eleventh-grade team of teachers who work with students in a criminal justice program may be grouped together as a Data Team even though they teach courses ranging from American literature to forensic science. Likewise, a ninth-grade team may work together to ease the transition from middle to high school for students and may include teachers of academics in addition to electives like physical education and computer technology. (However, the most common configuration of Data Teams at the high school level is by the specific course being taught, not across courses.)

See Exhibit 2.1 for an example of a horizontal Data Team.

A *vertical* team is so-named because it includes members from multiple grade levels. A common configuration of this kind of team occurs at the middle or high school level as a department team. So a middle school English language arts Data Team might include all the teachers of that subject in grades 6, 7, and 8. This type of team would select an identified student learning need that impacts each grade level,

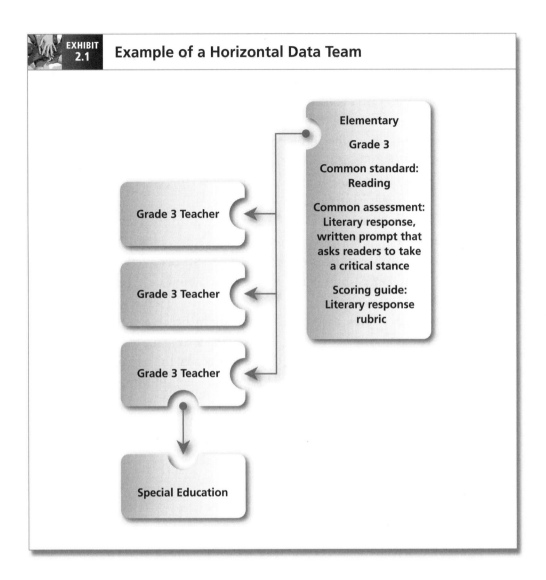

EXHIBIT 2.1 Example of a Horizontal Data Team

Elementary

Grade 3

Common standard: Reading

Common assessment: Literary response, written prompt that asks readers to take a critical stance

Scoring guide: Literary response rubric

Grade 3 Teacher

Grade 3 Teacher

Grade 3 Teacher

Special Education

such as making valid inferences when reading or acquiring necessary academic vocabulary for further study in the discipline. Again, the need drives the creation of the assessment that the team uses.

An example of a high school vertical team could be all teachers who teach algebra I, across the grade levels. This type of team could first zero in on any needs the students demonstrate with the prerequisite skills for success in the course. Later, the team would focus on the critical concepts and skills necessary in this foundational math course. Ideally, students at all grade levels who are enrolled in algebra I would achieve success by the end of the year.

See Exhibit 2.2 for an example of a vertical Data Team.

A *specialist* team is formed based on a special need that students have demonstrated. For example, the freshman year of high school is often a difficult transition time for students, so a ninth-grade transition team that consists of various adults who interact with those students could be formed. In this case, the team's data may come from periodic surveys of students and from information on attendance, tardiness, discipline, and course grades. The team could include the ninth-grade English and math teachers, the counselor and administrator who work most closely with ninth-grade students, and other professionals who may be important to the students' success, like the physical education teacher and the school social worker. Another type of specialist team at the high school level might be for seniors, focusing on college and career readiness.

At the middle school level, a specialist team might be formed to focus on eighth-grade students who are overage or otherwise at risk of failing. This team would closely monitor multiple sources of data on these students and take action in response so that the largest number of students possible would enter high school prepared for success.

At the elementary level, a specialist team might be created to monitor the progress of all children who are reading below grade level. This team could include representative teachers from each grade, the literacy coach, the school media specialist, and others who would enact strategies to support these students—strategies that

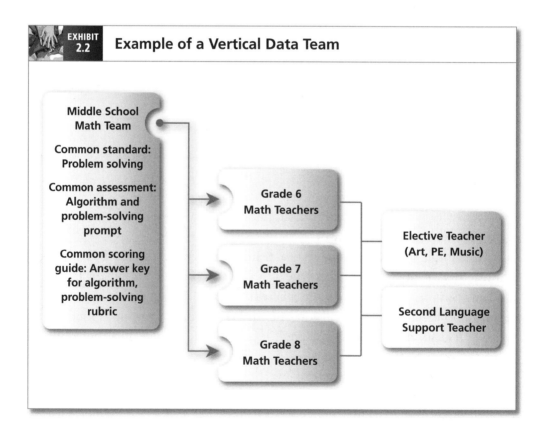

EXHIBIT 2.2 Example of a Vertical Data Team

complement what the grade-level Data Teams and school administrators do to move those same students ahead in their reading.

See Exhibit 2.3 for an example of a specialist Data Team.

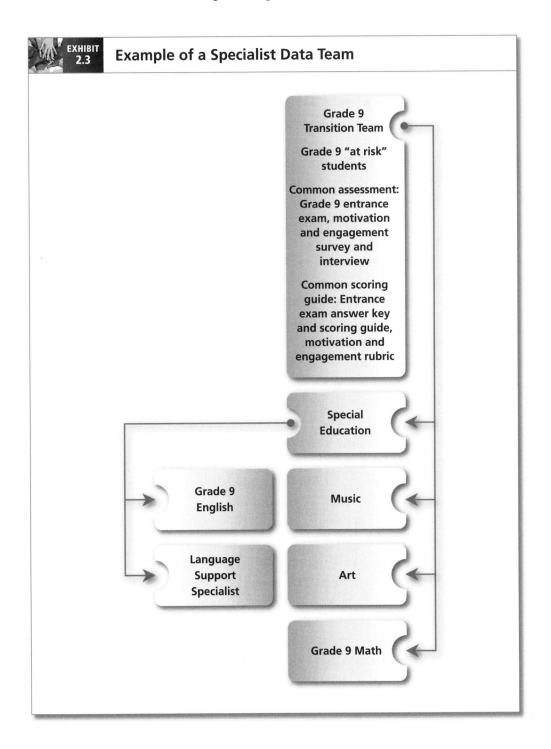

EXHIBIT 2.3 **Example of a Specialist Data Team**

What Roles Do People Play on Data Teams?

Every Data Team needs a leader and members. There are several types of responsibilities that team members can take on. These responsibilities are often determined based on the size of the team and the strengths of the members—but regardless of these factors, and others that may be in play, several key responsibilities must be met at all times in order for a team to function effectively.

Some roles are optional, but the one role that must be filled is the Data Team leader. This person can volunteer for the role, be appointed by the principal, or be selected by the team. This role may also rotate among members, but if it does rotate all members of the team must be well equipped to serve.

The Data Team leader must be both a good listener and an effective facilitator of dialogue. He is not necessarily a person who fills another leadership role (like department chairperson or grade-level team leader). In many cases, the teachers who fill those roles already have many demands on their time, so they may not be a good fit—or some of their other obligations will need to be reduced.

Data Team leaders are not pseudoadministrators, meaning that they do not evaluate the performance of colleagues or supervise those colleagues in any way. The Center recommends that all Data Team leaders meet with the principal at least monthly to debrief and discuss what is happening with the teams, but this is an information-sharing meeting, not a time to critique one's peers. It is important that all members of a Data Team understand the leader is primarily a facilitator, not an evaluator in any sense of the word.

Data Team leaders must sincerely believe that all students can achieve at high levels with the appropriate support from adults. They must also be willing to challenge the views and assumptions of their colleagues in order to strategize and innovate so that all students experience academic success. Because they serve as leaders in innovation, they should be well informed about instructional strategies. Often principals and central office administrators target Data Team leaders to attend conferences and engage in other forms of professional development so that they can serve as knowledgeable resources for their colleagues.

Frequently, other roles or responsibilities include recorder, data technician, data wall curator, timekeeper, and focus monitor. The recorder takes notes at the meeting and disseminates them to the entire team and the administration. The data technician collects data and prepares it for sharing with the team. A data wall curator is charged with displaying the ongoing results within the school. A timekeeper monitors the time that each step takes at the meeting and helps to ensure the team has time to complete the entire process. The focus monitor works with the timekeeper to ensure that dialogue stays tightly focused on teaching and learning.

All members of the team must play the crucial role of engaged participant. While it is generally up to the leader to set the agenda, communicate the meeting time and place to everyone, and conduct the discussion, each person must make meaningful contributions and commit to the strategies once those strategies are determined.

Team members should also be prepared to listen respectfully, pose questions to push the group's thinking forward, and take on portions of the group's work, like maintaining Data Team records, making copies of the common assessment, and researching research-based instructional strategies.

How Do Data Teams Determine a Focus to Begin Their Work?

Once teams have been configured, and after all Data Team members understand the norms for Data Team meetings, the work of data analysis begins.

Often, an entire faculty begins the Data Teams journey together by examining the various types of data about student achievement that is available. This data usually contains several years' worth of state test scores, in addition to system benchmark data and other information that schools are required to monitor. This data is almost always what we at The Center call "effect data," meaning that it shows an "end result" or performance at a given moment in time.

With all the effect data in hand, the faculty members "drill down" to find possible areas of focus. The "drilling" process always includes examining test data at the strand or subskill level and using disaggregated data to ensure that the performance of all subgroups of learners is clearly understood.

Let's examine a middle school example. Perhaps the school has had a history of students not doing well on the state's English language arts assessment; in fact, only about 40 percent of their students score proficient or above. When the data is examined more closely, two strands of the reading portion of the assessment seem to be the areas in which students struggle the most (vocabulary in context and inferences). After those two strands are identified, educators examine the various subgroups of students who don't do well in these strands. Perhaps they find that only 15 percent of African American males and only 10 percent of English Language Learners score proficient or higher in the two strands. These two groups of nonproficient students are both fairly equally distanced from the proficient scores in both vocabulary and inference.

The faculty in this example would now have ideas about where to begin. First, it seems that most students struggle with the reading portion of the state's English language arts assessment. More specifically, the skills of determining word meaning in context and making valid inferences are the two areas in which students seem to struggle the most. Data Teams could use these two areas to frame their work. So, the sixth-grade team might decide to tackle inferences. They would then meet, examine what their grade-level, prioritized standards say about inferences, and break those standards into manageable "chunks" appropriate for short-cycle assessments. The team would then create the pre- and post-assessment to be used to check students' inference skills. The eighth-grade team might decide that the vocabulary needs of their students are more urgent and act in a similar way to begin the Data Teams process.

Another common way to start Data Teams is for the principal or the building leadership team to have conducted an analysis of multiple years of data and to select a broad area in which teams should initially focus (we at The Center call this a Decision-Making-for-Results process). Often this same area of focus appears prominently as a goal in the school improvement plan. For example, an elementary school might have shown improvement in its state math test scores for the past few years. However, student proficiency in one area of math, problem solving, has not risen. So the principal in this particular school could ask all the Data Teams to begin their work by focusing on mathematics problem solving as appropriate for their grade levels.

Rarely are Data Teams effective in schools when they have little direction from the administration. The teams are formed and are then told to go forth and do the work. These teams often flounder because of a lack of understanding of how to examine multiple sources of large-scale data and make it relevant to the group of students with whom they work. However, because some teams given inadequate direction have a dynamic and dedicated mix of individuals, they can still achieve success.

In the upper elementary, middle school, and high school grades, teachers often use common unit or chapter tests. While the ideal is for Data Teams to select or generate their own pre- and post-assessments, some Data Teams start the work with assessments they have already been using. These teams are often the ones who have received limited support at the beginning of the process or who have not had time "up front" to prioritize standards, develop curriculum, and create common formative assessments. The important thing to remember is that they are beginning the process. With time, such teams become increasingly assessment-savvy.

How Do Administrators Interact with Data Teams?

The success of instructional Data Teams in a building depends on the full support and active involvement of administrators.

Through their words and actions, administrators set the tone for Data Teams in the building. Administrators must ensure that the expectations for Data Teams are clear and that teams have the conditions and resources they need to conduct their meetings effectively. They should provide dedicated time for teams to meet, resources and tools to help make data analysis easier, and points of contact if there are problems.

Administrators must also interact with the teams and the team leaders frequently and in substantive ways so that all teams become high performing. All agendas and minutes or notes from the meetings should be shared with administrators. These documents may be shared in hard copy or electronically or housed in a data notebook that the administrators have access to at all times. The most successful implementations of Data Teams occur where principals actively monitor the work of the teams through studying the minutes, providing feedback to teams, conducting frequent classroom visits, and meeting with Data Team leaders.

Some administrators rotate among Data Team meetings as they occur, or hold scheduled Data Team meetings in a central location, like the school library, so that they can be readily available as an additional facilitator for all teams. Others divide Data Teams up, with certain teams falling under the guidance of each building administrator. In those cases, the designated administrators regularly attend the meetings of their teams and support the work in other ways, too, such as assisting with team-based professional development and acquiring helpful resources. While Data Team meetings are teacher led and learning driven, administrators serve in a critical monitoring and guiding role.

Face-to-face communication between team members and administrators is critical. The Center recommends that the principal meet with all Data Team leaders at least once a month in order to stay abreast of the progress of the teams and to provide needed support. Additionally, in an aligned system, the data and analysis that are produced in the Data Teams process are predictors of state test results. It's critical for the principal to closely monitor the work of the teams in order to chart a course to success on summative measures.

Some schools, particularly large high schools, assign administrators to certain teams so that those administrators serve as a first point of contact. The appointed administrators can then sit in on Data Team meetings, visit teachers' classrooms to observe the instructional strategies in action, and provide updates to the other administrators.

Because Data Team leaders do not act in a supervisory or evaluative capacity, the observations of administrators are very important. And while administrators should visit Data Team meetings, they serve as "ad hoc" members, meaning they generally do not lead those meetings but engage as a participant would. (Problematic situations in which administrators might consider taking a more active role in Data Team meetings are discussed in Chapter 8.)

How Is the Work of Data Teams Communicated within the School?

Every time a Data Team meets, minutes should be taken. These minutes should be distributed to all team members and to administrators. Also, most Data Teams maintain a binder in which agendas, minutes, and copies of the common assessments are stored. Usually these binders are kept in a place that only adults have access to, but they are available for any teacher, paraprofessional, or administrator to peruse.

Some schools have dedicated folders on their main server to which all Data Teams post their results in either Word or Excel format. It is important when posting results electronically in public folders that a data technician or recorder for each team ensures the posted documents are read-only so that they are not inadvertently changed by someone who reads the file.

The Center encourages Data Teams to openly display their results within the school. Displays should provoke professional dialogue and invite celebration. Thus, results should be posted by team, not by individual teacher, and student names should never be used.

Results can be communicated with simple tables, charts, or graphs. Both pre-assessment and post-assessment data should be included, along with some kind of short explanation of the strategies that led to the post-assessment results.

Team and grade-level results can be posted in classrooms, hallways, the main office, or faculty workrooms, as determined by the administration or building leadership team. At one elementary school in California, a section of the cafeteria wall is where teams post their results, and teachers and students engage in active support of each other with cheers and chants at the wall (personal communication, Jenny Delmarter, Edison School District).

How Is the Work of Data Teams Communicated to Stakeholders outside the School?

Some school systems with which The Leadership and Learning Center has worked conduct Data Fairs, or what we call the "Science Fair for Grown-ups." These celebratory events may occur any time during the school year and provide rich information about the strategies employed in each school (Reeves, 2010, p. 140).

In a system-wide Data Fair, each school would have a three-panel display board that includes external data on the left panel. This is information from state tests, system assessments, and other assessments that were not designed by Data Teams. There may also be some brief narrative. For example, a statement like this could appear on the left panel: "82 percent of our students are proficient and higher in mathematics according to the current state test scores, and 75 percent are proficient according to the district benchmark test. Our last three years of data show consistent progress on both state and district measurements, with particular gains in mathematics problem solving."

On the center panel of each school's display, the school provides information about internal data—that is, the teaching practices associated with the selected content area (e.g., mathematics), followed by another brief narrative, such as the following: "The charts show that the number of math assessments, including constructed-response (writing) items, has increased significantly in the past year. Those assessments have emphasized mathematics problem solving as aligned with our state test. The charts also show an increased focus on mathematics vocabulary, with each teacher using vocabulary journals and nonlinguistic representations throughout the year to help students learn the most important terms."

The right panel of each display contains inferences and conclusions that answer the question, "Why are we getting the results we are?" To follow the example from above, this panel could say something like the following: "Our analysis suggests that increased writing in math and the focus on vocabulary instruction have both been effective strategies to improve student performance. Therefore, we have planned to expand these strategies next year by requiring students to write a reflection on their math learning each week and by having interactive word walls to highlight the important vocabulary terms. We remain very concerned about the 11 percent of students who are not proficient on the math portion of the state tests, and have developed intervention plans for each of these students."

At the Data Fair, educators and invited guests circulate and interact with the educators who are stationed at each display. Parents, board of education members, and central office administrators who have participated in Data Fairs all over the country have reported to Center associates that it is a very informative and rewarding experience.

Other ways to report on the achievement of incremental goals by Data Teams is to highlight them on the school Web site or in the parent newsletter. Again, the intent is to celebrate the gains being made, and results are reported by team or grade level, never by teachers' names.

Conclusion

Data Teams can be formed in multiple ways, depending on the unique needs and challenges at each school site. Each member of a Data Team plays an important role. Effective Data Team leaders are critical to the success of Data Teams. When beginning their work, Data Teams examine various sources of student achievement data before determining a focus for their work. Administrators also play an important role in Data Teams implementation; highly engaged administrators generate success. The valuable work of Data Teams should be communicated both internally and externally through such mechanisms as Data Team minutes and Data Fairs.

CHAPTER 3

Step by Step—
An Introduction to the Process
Followed in Data Team Meetings

The right kind of continuous, structured teacher collaboration improves the quality of teaching and pays big, often immediate, dividends in student learning and professional morale in virtually any setting.

—SCHMOKER, 2006

During a pre-instruction or post-instruction Data Team meeting, team members follow a five-step process that guarantees they will take specific actions to address the "real-time" learning needs of their students as reflected in the work from the most recent common formative assessment task. Between these Data Team meetings, monitoring meetings are held. At these meetings, the crucial sixth step of monitoring and evaluation occurs and allows teams to make midcourse corrections as needed.

This chapter will focus on the five steps that occur in each pre- or post-instruction meeting. Chapter 7 will focus on each of the five steps in much greater detail. The sixth step of monitoring and evaluation will be covered in Chapter 4.

ESSENTIAL QUESTIONS

What constitutes "data" for a Data Team meeting?

What do Data Teams do when they meet?

How is student work used in a Data Team meeting?

Why are SMART goals an important part of Data Team meetings?

Why must teams select common instructional strategies?

Why must results indicators be discussed?

How are the five steps adapted for the unique needs of teams?

What Constitutes "Data" for a Data Team Meeting?

While the work of Data Teams in any school often begins with a careful analysis of large-scale data that is available (such as state or system standardized test data), *this is not the kind of data that teams continue to examine.* Data Teams examine data derived from common, teacher-created assessments, which are administered to all the students represented by the teachers on the team.

When teams begin the Data Team cycle, they first determine an area of need— or, as discussed in the previous chapter, building leaders may determine an initial focus area and ask teams to operate within that area. After each team determines the specific content or skills for which they will collect data, and after they have completely "unwrapped" the accompanying standards, they must create a common formative assessment they will administer to check student proficiency in the targeted content or skills.

This teacher-created assessment may consist of entirely original items, or of items available through sources like online databases and ancillary materials, or of a combination of original and nonoriginal items. *However, it's critical that the team agrees that the items on the assessment accurately measure the "unwrapped" standards.* The assessment should, overall, answer the question, "What must students master as a result of our teaching?"

The team should agree on what constitutes correct answers for each item and on what proficiency is for the entire assessment. For example, an assessment about specific, grade-level writing conventions might include five multiple-choice questions that ask students to correct errors in the given sentences. The assessment might also include a short, constructed-response item for which students must write several complete, correct sentences. Overall proficiency, or "meeting standard" level for this assessment, could be for a student to get at least four of the multiple-choice items correct, in addition to scoring proficient on the constructed-response item. The team would need to create or use an appropriate rubric for the constructed-response item.

The Data Teams assessment is administered *prior to instruction,* at the beginning of a unit or chapter. This is generally called the pre-assessment. The results from this pre-assessment become the first data set the team uses in the five-step Data Team meeting.

After the pre-instruction Data Team meeting occurs, team members implement the agreed-upon instructional strategies and monitor their efforts. When teams are just beginning to operate, they often apply only one or two research-based instructional strategies, sometimes only in whole-class instruction. As teams refine their work to improve their performance, they often determine differentiated strategies and services for various proficiency levels and subgroups of students. These groups are determined based on the current performance level of each child as shown on the most recent assessment. Data Teams also refine their work as they become more effective by matching instructional strategies to key individual students, like those who are still in need of intensive intervention after a post-assessment.

At the end of any unit, chapter, or designated "chunk" of learning, students take a post-assessment. This measure is either an exact, repeat administration of the pre-assessment or an alternate form of that assessment. The data from the post-assessment is the next "fresh" data set the team has available to act upon and thus becomes a starting point for the next five-step meeting.

"Data" from these assessments consists not only of the number and percentage of students who met the stated standard of proficiency but also of information gleaned from student responses. Short and extended constructed-response items often yield richer data for a team to discuss, but even when an assessment consists only of selected-response, or "one right answer," items, teams can analyze error patterns and conduct item analyses. *What is most important to remember is that the errors lead teachers to change their instructional practices.*

Assessment design is in the team's hands. Team members should be comfortable that each assessment accurately measures what they intended to measure. The data that results, whatever form it may be in, then anchors Steps One and Two of the five-step meeting process at the next meeting.

Assessments won't necessarily be of the best quality initially in a Data Team's work; however, it is critical that teams start assessing student learning immediately. The information gained from common assessments, even if not "perfect," can be acted upon intelligently so that student learning is increased.

What Do Data Teams Do When They Meet?

After a pre-assessment has been administered, the Data Team convenes to discuss the results and act upon them. This meeting is called the "before-instruction collaboration meeting" or, more concisely, the pre-instruction meeting.

These five steps are followed at that particular meeting:

1. **The team collects and charts (or displays) the data.** Members examine the number and percentage of students proficient and nonproficient both teacher by teacher and for the entire team. They may also drill down into the data in order to increase clarity about exactly which students are struggling, which are close to proficient already, and which may need acceleration because they are at or beyond proficiency.

2. **The team analyzes the data and prioritizes needs.** The analysis should focus on student strengths and on urgent needs as evidenced in the student work. This step goes beyond labeling students and should lead to inferences about student performance. In other words, why are students performing the way they are? Such inferences are critical because later in the meeting team members must target specific learning needs and match instructional strategies to those needs *so that the highest number of students possible will achieve proficiency.* The ultimate concern is always what can be done to significantly increase student learning.

3. **The team sets a SMART goal.** The acronym SMART stands for specific, measurable, achievable, relevant, and timely. This goal is the growth target and clearly states the expected percentage of students who will be proficient and higher in the measured standards at the end of the designated instructional time.

4. **The team determines the instructional strategies they will implement in order to raise student proficiency.** The team should ask, "Which strategies will have the greatest impact on student learning based on the needs we identified in Step Two?" Another question that often deserves discussion in Step Four is "What strategies are individual teachers implementing with a high degree of success, and should these practices be replicated?" The team also agrees on how teachers will implement the strategies. This part of the discussion may include how instruction will be differentiated for students in various performance levels, such as "beyond proficient," "proficient," "close to proficient," "further from proficient but likely to be proficient after instruction," and "in need of intensive support." Again, not all teams are able to discuss various learning needs at this level of detail initially. *The important thing to remember about Step Four is that at least one research-based, likely-to-be-effective instructional strategy must be agreed upon and immediately implemented in order to enhance student learning.*

5. **The team determines results indicators.** Basically, results indicators state the evidence that the agreed-upon strategies are being implemented effectively. Results indicators describe the teacher behaviors that will be seen as the strategies are implemented, in addition to the student actions that provide evidence of the impact of the strategies on their learning.

Data Team members must leave this meeting knowing the SMART goal, what they will do to improve instruction, how they will monitor their own efforts, when and how the post-assessment will be administered, and when the next meeting will occur.

The next Data Team meeting at which data is analyzed is the meeting after the administration of the post-assessment. At this "after-instruction collaboration meeting," or post-instruction meeting, the same five basic steps are followed, but some steps are slightly different.

At Step Three, the team reviews its SMART goal(s) and determines whether to set a new goal(s) or to revise the current goal(s) because not enough students reached proficiency. If the team decides to move to a new focus area and a new goal because the earlier goal was achieved, then there are details that must be worked out about what the next pre-assessment will be, when and how it will be administered, and so on.

If the current goal was not yet achieved, then Step Four is also adapted. At this step, the teachers analyze their use of the agreed-upon instructional strategies. This analysis leads to the refinement of current strategies or the replacement of those strategies with new ones that the team predicts will be more effective. If different strategies were not previously employed for the various proficiency levels of students, then it is at this meeting that a differentiation discussion often occurs.

Monitoring meetings occur between the pre- and post-instruction meetings and can take several different forms. Because there is not pre- or post-assessment data to take through the five basic meeting steps at a monitoring meeting, specific steps or actions a Data Team might take differ from situation to situation. The main goals of a monitoring meeting are for the team to collectively reflect on their use of the agreed-upon strategies and to review student work samples (Leadership and Learning Center, 2010). The work samples may be drawn from the assessment or from an interim, classroom-based formative assessment. Teachers may also share their observations and anecdotal record-keeping at monitoring meetings. All information is shared and discussed in order for the team to collectively decide on any necessary modifications to instructional practice that will occur before the post-assessment is administered.

Multiple examples detailing the five steps are given in Chapter 7. The examples provided already are intended only to introduce the five steps in the context of the three basic types of Data Team meetings: before-instruction collaboration, after-instruction collaboration, and monitoring meetings.

How Is Student Work Used in a Data Team Meeting?

At Step Two of a before-instruction or after-instruction collaboration meeting, student work is examined closely so that team members can make valid inferences about what students know and can do—and about what challenges the students face in their learning.

Teachers ideally arrive at a Data Team meeting with all papers from the assessment already scored, using the team's agreed-upon proficiency criteria, answer key, or scoring guide. They should also already have their papers sorted into categories for the purpose of discussion. For the purpose of keeping the discussion focused and succinct, some teams even select specific work samples that illustrate common strengths, misunderstandings, or challenges.

At minimum, there should be two categories of student performance: students who are already at or beyond proficiency and students who are not yet proficient. Not yet proficient can be further categorized as the following: those who are close to proficiency, those who are further away but are predicted to become proficient, and those who will most likely need extensive support.

If individual teachers are not comfortable sorting the student work into all four categories prior to the team's dialogue, they should simply come to the meeting with student work sorted into the two broad categories (proficient and nonproficient) and be prepared to discuss the inferences they individually made during the scoring process. The team can then collaboratively group student work into more specific categories in order to best act on the needs they see reflected in the work.

As Data Teams become accustomed to working together and to developing high-quality formative assessments, they start to go into greater detail when examining student work at Step Two. Often they start learning more about how to best assess declarative knowledge (content-based) versus procedural knowledge (skills-based), how to increase the cognitive rigor of assessment items, and how to find evidence of student misunderstanding within the students' responses.

Teams also become increasingly sophisticated at determining what students really do know and what they really can do, regardless of issues that can sometimes cloud teachers' true understanding of student learning—like the acquisition of a new language, learning disabilities in written communication, or even something as surface-level as sloppy handwriting. When Data Teams put their heads together *frequently* to inspect student work, they grow in their capacity to "tease out" evidence of student learning while ignoring variables unimportant or unrelated to the "unwrapped" standards.

Why Are SMART Goals an Important Part of Data Team Meetings?

The third step of a before- or after-instruction Data Team meeting is the setting or revising of one or more SMART goals. The acronym *SMART* delineates several key concepts not only about Step Three but about Data Teams in general.

SMART goals are specific. They target a subject area, grade level, and student population. They are also measurable, meaning they specify the exact content or skills to be checked and describe the measurement instrument to be used. Achievable means that the goal states the expected percentage gains that will be realized after the instructional strategies are applied. One consideration here is the current performance of all students (Leadership and Learning Center, 2010). Relevancy is based on the fact that the learning target chosen is directly related to the students' most urgent needs. The last letter of the acronym stands for timely, meaning that the goal clearly states when the assessment will take place. The word *timely* also echoes the nature of the common formative assessments—they occur within fairly short spans of time.

Educators are often skilled in and comfortable with analyzing why students are struggling with learning content-area information or a given skill. They are less apt to set clear goals, determine specific timelines, and commit to action. In his article "Tipping Point: From Feckless Reform to Substantive Instructional Improvement" (2004, pp. 424–432), Mike Schmoker says, "the most productive thinking is continuous and simultaneous with action—that is, with teaching—as practitioners collaboratively implement, assess, and adjust instruction as it happens." Bemoaning the lack of student understanding or skill is only a first step; teachers must decide to do something in response, and the five-step Data Teams process is filled with action and the monitoring of action.

Step Three is crucial because it grounds the entire Data Teams process. It spurs teams to hold themselves accountable, and it makes incremental progress tangible. Without short-cycle, specific goals and the monitoring of progress in relation to those goals, collaborative teams may lose track of time or shift their focus from the most urgent student needs. Setting SMART goals prevents inertia and encourages both focus and action.

Why Must Teams Select Common Instructional Strategies?

Step Four of every before- and after-instruction collaboration meeting focuses on selecting instructional strategies that the entire team will use in order to increase student learning. These strategies are the prioritized, intentional adult actions that the team has collaboratively determined will have the greatest positive impact on learning.

Teams generally select from one to three research-based instructional strategies to implement. At minimum, the team must agree upon one. Teams that select more than three find that monitoring the effectiveness of too many actions becomes cumbersome.

Also, all team members must understand how to put the agreed-upon strategies into practice. If several strategies are selected, then the entire team needs time to discuss how the strategies will "play out" in each classroom and for each performance level of students. If different strategies are to be used with different groups of students, the team members must know exactly how to use all the strategies in addition to when and with whom to use the strategies. This level of detail can require lengthy discussion and even the modeling of strategies for each other.

The first consideration at Step Four should be to reflect on one's current practice and to ask, "What strategies could we employ immediately with the most students possible in order to change the results we are currently getting?" Consequently, Step Four should constitute a significant portion of any meeting but may be abbreviated in a post-instruction meeting during which a previously set SMART goal has been met. However, even in that situation, a thoughtful discussion of strategies that could be replicated and applied in the future should occur. In this way, teams proactively build effective instructional "toolboxes" that can be accessed throughout any given cycle of formative assessment.

The selection of common strategies does not prevent any teacher on the team from also employing "in the moment" and "just in time" strategies in the classroom as instruction occurs. More detail about team employment of effective strategies and how this process works in tandem with individual strategies appears in Chapter 8, Troubleshooting and Frequently Asked Questions.

Additionally, a thorough discussion of what high-performing Data Teams do for Step Four also appears in Chapter 7. Resources to help teams familiarize themselves with effective strategies are outlined in Chapter 8 and in the References list.

Why Must Results Indicators Be Discussed?

"Results indicators" are not just the improved student scores or performances. They are statements that clearly outline the adult behaviors that will be observed, the student actions that will be observed, and the change in student proficiency and understanding that is expected if the agreed-upon strategies are enacted.

Just like an athlete often uses visualization as he is practicing in order to envision his success, teachers must "see" in their minds how the strategies will occur and what will result from the use of the strategies. The results indicators are the verbal and written expression of the team's expected successes.

Here is an example. A middle school mathematics Data Team was trying to help their students improve in solving multistep word problems. One of the strategies agreed upon at Step Four of a meeting was the following: "Teachers will use a graphic organizer to help show students how to solve a multistep word problem using both computation and graphic representation."

For this particular strategy, possible results-indicator statements include the following: "More students will accurately solve multistep word problems." "More students will be able to write a short constructed response to a multistep word problem that includes the correct process steps and a correct explanation." "Each team teacher will model short constructed responses in mathematics, using the graphic organizers daily during the warm-up segment of instruction."

How Are the Five Steps Adapted for the Unique Needs of Teams?

The five steps that are followed in every meeting have resulted in success for thousands of teachers and students both in the United States and abroad. However, sometimes the steps need to be adjusted slightly to take into account the uniqueness of a particular system, building, group of students, or course.

One of the most common situations that Center associates have seen is the formation of a team that consists of teachers who teach various courses. Although this configuration is not recommended by The Center, it often occurs at the high school level because of a requirement for all teachers to be part of a Data Team in the school. For example, there may be a business department team, a vocational team, a foreign language team, and a physical education/driver's education team. These educators share neither students (like across an entire grade level) nor subject matter (each teacher teaches various courses, often single sections of each). This lack of commonality puts the team at a disadvantage from the beginning.

Some teams of this type have been successful, determining a common, cross-curricular focus like comprehending informational text, writing proficient essays, or using academic vocabulary relevant to the broad content area represented by the team. Remember that a successful Data Team is predicated upon the use of common assessment information; if a team cannot easily create common assessments, then the work of the team is stymied.

If a team such as this is formed and cannot agree on what to assess in common, then an adaptation can be adopted in which each teacher presents his own assessment information and the team focuses mostly on Step Four, working with each other to study and employ effective strategies. In this way, each teacher uses the five steps as an individual, reflective protocol to guide his work, but the Data Team meetings are spent on collaboration about instructional practice.

One high school team in Savannah, Georgia, used this kind of adaptation fairly effectively for a year. The team consisted of two ROTC instructors, an art teacher, and two foreign language teachers. The teachers each taught their own units and used their own assessments but met twice a month to share their progress and to improve their instructional delivery.

Another common situation, particularly in rural or especially small school systems, is one in which there is just one teacher of a course in the building. For example, there may be only one third-grade teacher, although there are two teachers at each grade level below because class sizes are kept very small; or at the high school level, there may be only one teacher of chemistry. How do "singleton" teachers use the Data Teams process?

Several solutions to the singleton question have been attempted by various systems The Center has consulted with in the past decade. One solution is to use technology to connect teachers of the same subject or course at different schools. They can use electronic bulletin boards, wikis, and other forums, in addition to e-mail and even videoconferencing, to collaborate. Of course, they still need to have common formative assessment data with which to work. If they have a common curriculum, secondary teachers often begin with a pre-assessment designed to cover the whole course, or perhaps just the first half of the course. If this kind of pre-assessment is not available or cannot be designed prior to the beginning of the school year, teachers may start the Data Teams process by using the textbook materials available for the first unit or first chapter. Often there are two forms of chapter tests, so one could be used for a pre-assessment and the other could be used for the post-assessment.

Another solution for singleton teachers is for systems to create times and structures for them to convene periodically. Some systems have required monthly professional development meetings for an hour or so after school or on early-release days. In such a setting, all the art teachers could meet in one location, all the band teachers could meet in another, and so on. Depending on the number of teachers of such subjects and on the specificity of the system's curriculum, different groups might be formed based on grade levels. So to continue the example, high school teachers of art I and art II might work together, while teachers of ceramics might work separately.

In order to best reach all students represented on a Data Team, at times Steps Two and Four might need to be adapted. So in the case where an ELL teacher of preproduction- or early-production-level students is part of a math team, the assessment may need to be given orally in the student's native language so that a true picture of the mathematics understanding emerges—not just a picture of the student not being able to decipher the language. Also in a case like this, the common instructional strategies would still be used but may need adaptation. If the team decides that using an acronym would help students remember the order of operations, members must remember that the acronym is language based and would therefore not be as helpful to ELL students as to native English speakers. So the ELL specialist on the team might need to develop a different acronym for his students or use a non-linguistic strategy instead, like a graphic organizer, a symbolic drawing, movement, or gestures to help students remember the same content as their peers who speak English proficiently.

Another question that often arises about the nature of the assessment and the selection of strategies is, "What about our identified special education students?" First, it's important to remember that a Data Team's overriding goal is to assess *grade-level* performance/proficiency. Most students who have Individualized Education Plans (IEPs) are working *below grade level,* and therefore instruction is modified in order for them to progress through the curriculum.

Instruction is modified, but the Data Teams assessment process generally is not modified. *Students with IEPs should take the same formative assessments as their peers so that the entire team understands their achievement in relation to grade-level standards.* Obviously, after a pre- and post-assessment cycle, these students often remain in the "need extensive support" category. Thus, they must continue receiving excellent instruction in the targeted content and skills. They are often targeted at this point for intensive intervention that the other students will not receive. This intervention will help them continue to work toward meeting grade-level standards.

If the special education students represented on a Data Team will not be tested on grade level when state or provincial assessments are given, then it is acceptable for the teacher monitoring the IEP goals to create adapted formative assessments. However, these assessments must reflect the same content and skills as the assessments the rest of the Data Team is using; they are simply "scaled down" in terms of grade level or as dictated in the IEP.

It is also acceptable in the regular classroom situation for a student with an IEP to receive the same accommodations on a Data Team assessment that he would receive on state or provincial assessments. However, again, *the overriding purpose behind Data Team assessments is to determine how well all students are doing in relation to the end-of-year or end-of-course standards and proficiency levels.* This simple fact must remain clearly in focus when determining how to handle special education students as part of the Data Teams process.

Often the special education teacher who is part of a Data Team is an expert in instructional strategies and is a valuable resource for everyone at Step Four. So any special education teacher who is part of a Data Team should actively participate in meetings and not work in isolation, even if he must adapt the formative assessments, SMART goals, or strategies for his students. The goal for the entire team remains the same: help as many students as possible meet the standards.

CHAPTER 4

Introduction to the Crucial Sixth Step—Monitoring and Evaluating

Because of the Data Teams process, our culture, our values and beliefs, and the actions and behaviors of staff members have changed. We've experienced a shift in focus from teacher needs to student needs.

—Jeffrey Keller, in Anderson, 2010

Many educators are familiar with the saying, "What gets monitored gets done." In the schools and systems where Data Teams have been most successful, this statement certainly applies. In those places, Data Team members, administrators, and other school personnel are continuously aware of the goals, strategies, and results of Data Teams.

This chapter provides the rationale for and explanation of the sixth step of Data Teams, the monitoring that occurs both during meetings and between meetings as a part of a continuous improvement cycle.

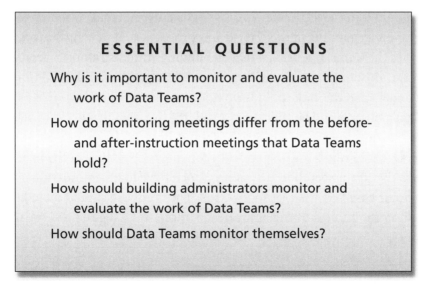

ESSENTIAL QUESTIONS

Why is it important to monitor and evaluate the work of Data Teams?

How do monitoring meetings differ from the before- and after-instruction meetings that Data Teams hold?

How should building administrators monitor and evaluate the work of Data Teams?

How should Data Teams monitor themselves?

Why Is It Important to Monitor
and Evaluate the Work of Data Teams?

In the places where Data Teams have been most successful, principals, content-area supervisors, instructional coaches, and central office administrators regularly visit Data Teams during scheduled meeting times (White Paper Series, Fort Bend Independent School District, http://leadandlearn.com/sites/default/files/FBISD-White-Paper.pdf). These visits serve several purposes.

First, the frequent presence of central administration or content-area supervisors clearly communicates the priority placed on the Data Teams process. When administrators and academic support personnel are out in school buildings to see Data Teams in action, it becomes apparent to all involved that the work of Data Teams collaboration is valued.

Second, district leaders need to monitor the degree to which Data Team meetings actually occur. Research conducted by The Center over the past decade shows that more frequent Data Team meetings equal greater student success.

Third, visits by supervisory personnel from outside the school building provide opportunities for these system leaders to give specific feedback to building leaders about Data Teams implementation. It is often very helpful for a principal to utilize "another set of eyes" to watch the work of Data Teams and to help plan for specific professional development or for other needed supports.

Last, by observing Data Teams, system leaders can identify exemplary teams and can use these teams in internal professional development in a variety of ways. Some systems have videotaped the meetings held by such teams and have used these videos in presentations in order to help others understand the five-step meeting process, norms that help teams operate effectively, and so on.

At the building level, principals and assistant principals often have varying degrees of understanding of the Data Teams process—and varying degrees of interaction with the teams. It is critical that all building administrators understand their role in monitoring the work of Data Teams. Ideally, all building administrators should understand the concept of formative assessment in the Data Teams process. They should observe and be able to assist with the five steps that occur in before- and after-instruction meetings. Also, they should observe frequently in classrooms between Data Team meetings, specifically looking for evidence of the instructional strategies that team members are using. Specific feedback to individual teachers should occur based on the classroom visits. This feedback should include positive feedback on the success of the strategies in addition to suggestions for increased effectiveness (if applicable).

Administrators should also make a regular practice of reviewing Data Team minutes. These documents are particularly important pieces of evidence of collaboration if administrators are not able to actually be present in meetings for some reason over a period of time.

In sum, direct observation of Data Team meetings, observation of classroom instruction, review of Data Team minutes, and periodic meetings with Data Team leaders are the main sources of information for principals and assistant principals.

Many schools and systems have used rubrics that delineate the levels of performance for Data Teams. Central and building administrators can use these tools as they observe teams in meetings. Team members can also use these to monitor their own work. Examples of rubrics that two schools have used are reproduced in Exhibits 4.1 and 4.2.

How Do Monitoring Meetings Differ from the Before- and After-Instruction Meetings that Data Teams Hold?

The term *monitoring meeting* denotes a meeting during which Data Team members do not have new data from a recently administered common assessment. These monitoring meetings, then, may occur *between* the before- and after-instruction meetings, during the time in which the selected instructional strategies are being enacted, or *after* the after-instruction meetings in which teams may or may not have met a SMART goal and are determining their next steps.

The purpose of a monitoring meeting is to discuss the effectiveness of the strategies being used by team members. At least some of the results indicators that were determined earlier should be evident; if they are not, this could mean that the strategies need to be adjusted.

Basically, during a monitoring meeting, the Data Team needs to ask itself, "Are the strategies we selected having the desired impact on student learning? If so, how do we know? If not, what do we do next to ensure greater success?" In order to answer these questions, teachers must draw upon all their daily, formative assessment practices. They must reflect on the strategies they are using and what students are doing in response in order to come to monitoring meetings best prepared to discuss the current state of student learning.

At monitoring meetings, team members may also bring student work samples so these samples can be examined for evidence about the effectiveness of the instructional strategies. By using these samples and asking the questions noted previously, teams can make midcourse corrections if current strategies are not working as

EXHIBIT 4.1 | # The Five-Step Data Teams Process

Teachers collectively examine how well students are doing, relate this to how they are teaching, and then make midcourse corrections to help all students achieve high standards.

Exemplary (4)	Proficient (3)	Progressing (2)	Not Proficient (1)
All criteria for the proficient category have been successfully met. In addition: • Teachers explore and experiment with alternative combinations of Data Team practices to maximize student outcomes. Examples: (1) Meet twice a month to examine together how well students are doing, relate this to how teachers are teaching, and then make improvements. (2) Meet weekly during lunch to examine pacing and make adjustments to instruction. • The Data Teams process is considered an essential school practice, which enables teachers to share ideas and best practices to develop and continuously improve instruction.	• Teachers apply the Data Teams process smoothly with minimal management problems. • Teachers come together at least once monthly to examine data from teacher-created, common assessments. • Teachers analyze student strengths and challenges to provide direction and focus. • Teachers establish incremental goals directly related to annual school goals. • Teachers select common instructional strategies to improve current levels of achievement. • Teachers determine desired results indicators.	• Teachers manage the Data Teams process with varying degrees of efficiency. The flow of actions is often disjointed, uneven, or uncertain. • Staff members participate in the Data Teams process but may not get through all five steps. Findings generated by this process are beginning to influence classroom practices.	• Teachers take no discernible action toward learning about or using the Data Teams concept. • Some staff members participate in classroom research. The sharing of findings is largely informal. • Teachers seem more concerned with their own identity than with a sense of shared community. They still teach as "private practice." • Teachers rarely take time to share ideas and best lessons with their colleagues to develop and improve instruction.

expected. Those corrections may include any of the following, in addition to other actions that the team feels are appropriate:

- Modeling the strategies for each other to determine fidelity of implementation
- Adding another effective, research-based instructional strategy to those already being used
- Deleting or replacing an instructional strategy being used
- Reorganizing students for instruction based on their learning needs, as inferred from student work examined in the meeting
- Referring especially needy students for additional support (in addition to what the teachers are doing during class instruction)

How Should Building Administrators Monitor and Evaluate the Work of Data Teams?

If building-level administrators are not tightly connected to the Data Teams process, then Data Teams will not work.

The research is abundant and clear: most principals, both effective and ineffective, pay "lip service" to the innovations they are asked to implement. However, there is one important difference that separates the effective from the ineffective—*effective principals* closely monitor initiatives to ensure follow-through (Duke, 2007, pp. 35–37).

Center consultants Kris Nielsen and Barb Pitchford have discussed the responsibilities of principals in monitoring Data Teams in terms of the "four Cs." These four phrases nicely summarize what principals must do to get Data Teams up and running and to keep them humming along.

The first C is for "clear course." The building leader must communicate the mission of Data Teams and provide the time, structure, and resources necessary for them to operate.

The second C is for "constant feedback." Building administrators must observe Data Team meetings and provide formative feedback to the teams so they can operate more effectively. Just as with students who are learning something new, teachers new to Data Teams also need to receive feedback about what they are doing well. Feedback to the teams is just one type of feedback principals need to give; they also must provide individual feedback to teachers about the strategies in action.

The third C is for "course correction." Data Teams will not work perfectly right out of the gate. Administrators need to allow for teams to reach proficiency at

| EXHIBIT 4.2 | **Effective Data Team Collaboration** |

Standard	
EXEMPLARY	• Meeting starts and ends on time. • All teachers are present and on task. • Meetings are organized with clear objectives, and agendas are given in advance to members. • All teachers and leader come prepared with an advance copy of an agenda and needed materials/data. • Minutes are taken, clearly reflect the content of the meeting, and are distributed to all in a timely manner. • All teacher input is done in a respectful and open environment. All teachers are participating in focused discussions. All members feel valued and provide input or comment on the work at hand. • All discussions are based on standards, student work, common assessment results, knowledge of student performance, and improving student achievement. • There is a goal for the meeting to reach consensus, set the next agenda, and assign needed tasks and timelines for the next meeting, as needed. • There is agreement that products produced or decisions made will be evaluated to determine effectiveness and/or use for the future.
PROFICIENT	• Meeting starts and ends on time. • All teachers are present and on task. • Agendas/meetings are organized with clear objectives. • All teachers and leader come prepared with an advance copy of an agenda and needed materials/data. • Minutes are taken, generally clearly reflect the content of the meeting (but may be abbreviated), and are distributed to all. • Most teacher input is done in a respectful and open environment. Most teachers are participating in focused discussions. Most members feel valued and regularly provide input or comment on the work at hand. • Almost all discussions are based on standards, student work, common assessment results, knowledge of student abilities, and improving student achievement. Interruptions or distractions (e.g., bird-walk, side talk) may *seldom* occur, but members or leader quickly redirects discussion. • There is generally a goal for the meeting to reach consensus, set the next agenda, and assign needed tasks and timelines for the next meeting, as needed. • There is an understanding that products produced or decisions made will be evaluated to determine effectiveness and/or use for the future.

EXHIBIT 4.2	**Effective Data Team Collaboration** (continued)

Standard	
PROGRESSING	• Meeting generally starts and ends on time. • Some teachers are present and on task. • Agendas/meetings are not always organized or have clear objectives. Some time is wasted or unused. • Some teachers come prepared with needed materials or data. Leader does not always have materials/agenda ready or has to "hunt" down or ask more than once for needed information or data. • Minutes are taken, but do not generally clearly reflect the content of the meeting (unorganized/unclear). Minutes are not always distributed to all. • Teacher input is generally done in a respectful and open environment. Some members dominate the discussion or remain silent. Members may feel criticized, uncomfortable, or hesitant to provide input or comment on the work at hand. • Some discussions are based on standards, student work, common assessment results, knowledge of student abilities, and improving student achievement. Interruptions and distractions (e.g., bird-walk, side talk) frequently occur and sometimes distract members for extended periods of time. • Sometimes there is a goal for the meeting to reach consensus, set the next agenda, and assign needed tasks and timelines for the next meeting, as needed. • There is some understanding that products produced or decisions made will be evaluated to determine effectiveness and/or use for the future.
NOT MEETING STANDARDS	• Meetings do not generally start or end on time. • Few members are present or on task. • Agendas/meetings are generally unclear and unorganized. Leader is having a difficult time getting anything "meaningful" accomplished. • Neither members nor leader have needed materials and/or data for meetings. • Minutes are generally vague or missing. Minutes are not distributed. • Meetings are generally negative or unproductive. Teacher input is not solicited or offered. Members frequently dominate discussion or disengage altogether. Teachers commonly participate in off-topic discussions/behavior. • Few discussions are based on standards, student work, common assessment results, knowledge of student abilities, or improving student achievement. • Meetings seldom have as a goal to reach consensus, set the next agenda, and assign needed tasks and timelines for the next meeting, as needed. • There is disagreement on how or why products produced or decisions made should be evaluated or used in the future.

different rates and allow them to stumble or fail and then make corrections to their strategies.

The last C represents the reminder to "celebrate success." Teachers are often fearful in the beginning stages of Data Teams because they feel they will be treated punitively when students don't do well. Principals are urged to celebrate team successes —even small successes—and to avoid coming on too strongly with teachers whose students aren't performing quite as well as those in other classrooms.

How Should Data Teams Monitor Themselves?

When Data Teams are first established, each team must determine and agree to its own norms. In other words, how will they work together as a team? The norms are the behavioral expectations or "rules" that will be adhered to during meetings.

Many teams establish norms such as the following:

- Arrive for the meeting on time, with all needed materials.
- Stay on topic.
- Use active listening when others are speaking; do not interrupt.
- Adhere to the times established in the agenda.
- Reflect on your own practice and share ideas that move the group forward.
- Express concerns about the team's work in the meetings, not to others outside of the meetings who aren't on the team.
- Complete tasks as assigned.
- Once you commit to a strategy or other action in the team meeting, implement it.
- Celebrate the team's successes.

Effective Data Team leaders sometimes stop meetings if norms are violated and process the issue with the team. When this happens, norms may be reviewed to ensure understanding or adjusted for future meetings if the team so agrees.

If Data Team leaders or administrators want to collect formative data about the Data Teams process in a school, they can administer an anonymous survey, asking questions such as the following about the norms being used by the various teams:

- How often do our Data Team meetings start and end on time?
- How often do all members of my Data Team come prepared for the work that needs to be done?
- How well do I understand the Data Teams process?

- How well do I understand my role/responsibilities on the Data Team?
- In Data Team meetings, are my contributions valued?
- In Data Team meetings, are the contributions of all team members valued?

All members of a Data Team have joint responsibility for the effectiveness of the meetings that are held. Therefore, it is important that each Data Team spend time up front (prior to designing assessments and prior to conducting before- and after-instruction meetings) developing norms for the team's work.

For more in-depth guidance, refer to The Ten Norms of Data Team Work, initially developed by Center associate Raymond Smith, at the end of this chapter.

Conclusion

Monitoring and evaluation are critical to the work of Data Teams. Effective Data Teams are constantly monitoring both their own actions and student results in order to continuously improve teaching and learning.

THE TEN NORMS
OF DATA TEAM WORK

Behaviors That Develop Open Dialogue

1. Pausing: Pausing before responding or asking a question allows time for you to frame your own thoughts and responses to enhance dialogue, discussion, and decision making within the group.

2. Paraphrasing: Paraphrasing signals listening and helps one understand and support others' thoughts by clarifying, organizing, and extending their thinking. Use a paraphrase starter that is comfortable for you ("So...," "As you were saying...," or "You're thinking..."). Follow the starter with a paraphrase that helps members of the group understand, find meaning, and seek agreement.

3. Probing: Ask questions that clarify vague language, explore details, and generate clear examples. Use gentle, open-ended probes or inquiries such as, "Please say more...," or "I'm curious about...," or "I'd like to hear more about...," or "Then, are you saying...?"

4. Putting ideas out to be examined: Ideas are the heart of a meaningful dialogue. Label the intention of your comments. For example, you might say, "Here is one idea...," or "One thought I have is...," or "Here is a possible approach...." In dialogue, one submits one's best thinking, knowing that other people's reflections will help improve it rather than destroy it.

5. Paying attention to self and others: Meaningful dialogue is facilitated when each group member is conscious of self and of others and is aware of not only what he is saying but also how it is said and how others are responding. Pay attention to learning styles when planning for, facilitating, and participating in group meetings. Responding to others in their own language forms is one manifestation of this norm. You might say, "I know that you like to examine statistical data on things, so...," or "You care so much about how students react when we change our expectations...," or something similar to begin.

6. Presuming positive intentions: Assuming that others' intentions are positive promotes meaningful dialogue and eliminates unintentional put-downs. Using positive intentions in your speech is one manifestation of this norm. For example, you might say, "I know that we all want our students to do well in this next unit" or something similar.

7. Pursuing a balance between advocacy and inquiry: Pursuing and maintaining a balance between advocating a position and inquiring about one's own and others' positions enhances the group's development in becoming a community of learners.

Behaviors That Develop a Community of Learners

8. Perpetuating continuous learning: Learning is meaning-making, constantly testing, refining, and getting feedback on the improvements in one's own efforts as well as in the collective efforts of the team. Joining your thinking and feeling into a shared pool of meaning carries the group into new, deeper levels of understanding that no one individual could have foreseen. This is the ultimate goal of working together collaboratively.

9. Practicing assessment literacy: This means examining student performance results and making critical sense of the information. The team must act on this collective understanding by setting goals, identifying and implementing strategies, describing desired results, and monitoring improvement efforts in order to make the kinds of changes needed to increase student achievement in targeted areas. The five steps followed in most Data Team meetings help each member practice their assessment literacy skills.

10. Paying attention to the connections between teachers' development and students' development: Teacher development and student development are intertwined. In other words, the value of teacher development must ultimately be judged by whether these changes make teachers better for their students in ways that teachers themselves can see.

Source: Four Hats Seminars in El Dorado Hills, California. Adapted by Raymond Smith and Angela Peery as part of The Leadership and Learning Center's work in Elkhart Community Schools, Indiana. Also adapted from Garmston and Wellman (2002).

CHAPTER 5

We're a Team, Now What?
The Initial Challenges Teams Face

*Collaboration is a means to an end, not the end itself. In
many schools, staff members are willing to collaborate on
a variety of topics as long as the focus of the conversation
stops at their classroom door.*

—DuFour, DuFour, Eaker, and Many, 2006

Once Data Teams are formed, there is often a period during which teachers adjust
to working with each other in this new manner. Because Data Team meetings are
unlike the grade-level, team, and department meetings of the past, teachers may
need time to adjust. As with other workplace groups, Data Teams take different
amounts of time to adjust, based on many variables.

This chapter discusses common struggles that Data Teams sometimes face as
they are beginning their work. Additionally, the various roles that members fulfill
and the potential problems that occur in those roles are discussed. The examples are
not intended to be all-inclusive but are offered in order to illustrate situations that
may indeed occur in your own Data Teams journey so that you may reflect on the
scenarios presented and be proactive in your approach.

The Stages of Team Development

Bruce Tuckman, a psychologist, first proposed his model of group development in
the 1960s. His model includes stages called forming, storming, norming, and performing. He postulates that all these stages are necessary and must occur in order for
any team to deliver results. So while moving through these stages is necessary, the
progress is often frustrating for both team members and administrators alike. However, understanding the stages can be beneficial for anyone involved with the work
of Data Teams, just as understanding Piagetian psychology or Bloom's Taxonomy of
Educational Objectives is helpful when teaching students. Many Data Teams with
whom I have consulted over the past five years have found that viewing the devel-

opment of their own teams through the lenses of Tuckman's work provides insight and affirmation.

Briefly, the forming stage of team development involves individuals trying to get along and avoid conflict. This stage often manifests itself as newly formed Data Teams busy themselves with organizational and logistical tasks, such as deciding where and when to meet and figuring out how to keep records like meeting minutes and data displays. Team members also spend time getting better acquainted with each other on a personal level. This stage is characterized by little work of significance; it is basically a "getting to know you" time.

Data Team leaders, instructional coaches, and administrators often grow impatient during this forming phase because they want each team to focus immediately on the student learning needs. However, a team cannot effectively address student learning needs until they have experienced the forming phase. The frustration team members and others may feel lies in the amount of time that it takes for some teams to successfully navigate this initial stage. Some teams pass though it in one or two meetings, while others take months. Like an algebra problem, the mix of friendships, personalities, and experience on each team creates a different formula for the length of the forming stage.

The next stage is called storming. In this stage, team members turn their attention to the problems that must be solved—for Data Teams, that means the student learning challenges that must be addressed. Tuckman's theory posits that some groups move through this stage very quickly, while others never leave it.

Some Data Teams remain in the storming phase, unfortunately, for an entire school year. Data Team leaders, instructional coaches, and administrators from both the building and system levels often try to intervene if this stage appears to last too long. Sometimes these efforts work with the existing team members, but in other cases the configuration of the team has to be changed. A change in team membership is an extreme solution but is one that is sometimes cautiously exercised by administrators.

Storming includes team members presenting their own views, which sometimes lead to controversy or conflict because they may differ drastically from the views of teammates. On some Data Teams, teachers may express ideas about student learning capabilities that are offensive to other members, such as, "Those particular kids will never be able to learn this. They just don't have what it takes. Why don't we just move on?" Another common problem during the storming stage is when one or two members share their instructional strategy ideas and don't entertain the suggestions of others; for example, "Here's the way to teach that. I've taught it that way for years and it's the only way the kids get it. I don't see why we're wasting time trying to come up with other methods." These kinds of statements prolong the storming stage because they don't encourage dialogue.

Those in supervisory, coaching, or team leadership positions can help teams move through the storming phase by guiding the dialogue. They can model effective ways to present ideas and can take statements such as the ones given previously and paraphrase them so that they become less definitive and more inviting. Many Data Team leaders grow frustrated during the storming phase, as they feel ill-equipped to handle the strong emotions that may be displayed by their colleagues. Data Team leaders who do grow frustrated need additional support from administrators or outside experts. Some Data Teams actually study information about group development prior to beginning the meeting cycle so that they are prepared for what's ahead.

The next stage in team development is norming. In this sometimes long-awaited stage, the team manages to have a shared goal and a consensual plan for reaching it. Team members have learned that sometimes they have to forego their own ideas, or at the very least find ways to combine their ideas with the ideas of others. In this stage, agreement is reached fairly easily, whereas in earlier stages, it was not.

In the norming stage, members have all taken responsibility and are keeping their commitments. They are all working toward the common good. From this point forward, a Data Team can be highly effective.

The last stage teams reach is the stage called performing. High-performing teams function interdependently and are able to do what's required with ease. Team members are motivated to do the work of the group, and direct supervision or guidance from outside members (like administrators) is not necessary. These are the teams that meet even when they don't have to. They enjoy and learn from their collaboration and feel that their teaching would not be as effective without it. The performing stage is the desired state for all Data Teams, because it is in this state that students can benefit the most.

The Differences between Elementary and Secondary School Data Teams

Many elementary teachers are accustomed to meeting in grade-level teams for various purposes: to discuss discipline issues; to plan class activities, including participation in art, music, and physical education; to share resources; to plan lessons and interventions; to monitor student achievement data; and so on. The difficult part for elementary teachers is to table discussions about issues that are not part of the five steps for other meetings, not Data Team meetings.

Because elementary teachers have often met as grade levels to do much of the work that is required, to conduct meetings focused only on current student achievement and how to change instruction to improve that achievement seems somewhat foreign or uncomfortable to them. In my own work with dozens of elementary Data Teams across the country, I have often noticed that conversations may gravitate to issues unrelated to instruction, such as student behavior, student absenteeism, or student and family illnesses, thereby lessening the time that can be allotted to discussion of instructional strategies. Of course, skillful Data Team leaders or ad hoc team members like administrators or instructional coaches are usually adept at getting the conversation back on track. With the heightened focus on student achievement because of No Child Left Behind and other legislation in the past few years, however, many elementary Data Teams start their work highly focused. My observations are offered only as a caution.

Some elementary teams decide to meet once a week as a Data Team and add an additional weekly or bimonthly meeting to handle other issues like the topics mentioned previously, which are valid topics for educators to discuss, obviously. Some Data Teams with whom I've worked meet weekly to conduct the steps of the Data Teams process and decide to handle unrelated items via e-mail and informal conversations throughout the day. These teams generally get excited about the results they are seeing and choose to devote more and more time to examining their students' work and to adjusting their own instructional strategies.

In secondary schools, especially comprehensive high schools, finding times for Data Teams to meet can seem daunting. If teams are formed by course, and teachers of the same course can be scheduled with a common planning period, this can easily become the time for Data Team meetings to occur. This is an ideal situation to set secondary teachers up for success from the very beginning of Data Teams work in a building.

In schools where it is not possible to schedule teachers for common planning, early-release days are often utilized for Data Teams. Also, principals who have traditionally held weekly faculty meetings have sometimes reduced these to two per month so that the other two time periods are used for Data Teams.

Once logistics are determined, secondary Data Teams can begin meeting, but often these meetings differ from those of elementary teams quite dramatically. Many secondary teachers have worked in a more isolated and autonomous fashion than have their elementary school peers, and this lack of experience with collaborative dialogue sometimes prevents them from "opening up" much at first.

The Critical Role of the Data Team Leader

Data Teams are collaborative in the best sense of the word: team members ideally "co-labor" in order to make instructional decisions that positively impact the learning of every student. However, particularly in the early stages of Data Teams work, the team leader plays a crucial role as the purpose and norms are established.

Data Team leaders may volunteer, apply, or be appointed by the administration. Those selected should have a strong understanding of standards and assessment, know how to analyze various forms of student achievement data, be familiar with research-based instructional strategies, and be able to facilitate meetings well. They should be respected as teacher-leaders in the building and should not be afraid to challenge commonly held beliefs if necessary. Data Team leaders must believe that all students can learn if provided adequate time and ideal conditions; they must also believe that teachers can continue to grow professionally throughout their careers.

The main responsibilities of a Data Team leader are to set the agenda for each meeting, ensure that all members know the agenda as well as where and when to meet, and, obviously, run the meeting as it occurs. The Center recommends that Data Team leaders meet with the principal or building leadership team once a month to debrief and make recommendations, so this is an additional responsibility. Data Team leaders must also ensure that minutes or notes are taken in each meeting and that these are distributed to all stakeholders; generally, the role of recorder is delegated to one person on the team, or this role rotates among members, as does the role of timekeeper.

Administrators should seek to remove any unnecessary duties from teachers selected to be Data Team leaders. On many campuses, Data Team leaders are also provided with small stipends or other perks in order to thank them for the important job they do. Perks may include low-cost options such as sending each Data Team leader to a conference, or no-cost options such as trading time on campus for time off campus (during prep periods or in-service days, for example).

The biggest challenge that Data Team leaders face is in their interactions with colleagues. It is imperative that all educators in the building understand that Data Team leaders are not pseudoadministrators. They are not serving in an evaluative or supervisory role but in a facilitative one. Thus, the Data Team leaders must be able to cultivate strong relationships with both their peers and their supervisors. So, while asking probing questions of their peers during meetings, they must remain neutral and nonjudgmental. And while sharing information with supervisors, they must strive to report facts and allow the supervisors to make the inferences and determine future actions.

Sometimes, well-intentioned administrators seek information from Data Team leaders that places the leaders in the difficult position of evaluating a teammate's performance. If this happens, the team leader must be as diplomatic as possible but resist falling into the trap. Minutes from meetings, data displays, and objective information shared in the monthly meetings of team leaders and administration should provide the administrators with plenty of material from which to generalize about any given teacher's performance. Principals should gather additional information from classroom observations, both formal and informal, and from conversations with members of the teams.

When Data Team leaders aren't skillfully navigating their relationships with their administrators, they may find themselves redefining their relationships with their teammates. At times, other members on the team may feel nervous about sharing the results from their classes for fear that their results aren't as good as the results of the rest of the team members. They may also be reluctant to share their teaching practices, for fear that the practices will be considered "not good enough" by their peers—or, contrarily, for fear that their teammates will think they are being braggarts. The Data Team leader must be alert to all the intriguing subtleties of human behavior that can prevent a team from reaching high performance.

Every building has those teachers on the faculty who would make excellent Data Team leaders. The challenge is to support them so that they don't "burn out" early in the process as teams move through the forming and storming stages.

Data Team leaders must also remember not to put too much pressure on themselves. They are not responsible for the work that their teammates are supposed to do—nor are they responsible for their teammates' behavior in meetings. They are responsible only for trying to facilitate the meetings and communicate between meetings as best they can to keep the team moving forward in the best interest of students.

Other Members of the Team

Every Data Team member must make the commitment to serve as an engaged participant. For some, this commitment is hard to make and even harder to live up to fully as meetings begin to occur.

Some teachers feel that they are being personally scrutinized as they open up their practice by sharing assessment ideas and assessment results with others. They also may be hesitant to discuss instructional strategies that they have used previously or suggest ideas about changes in instructional strategies. If Data Teams are implemented in a building where a collaborative culture has not been created or sustained, teachers may be very reluctant, especially initially, to participate in true dialogue about teaching and learning.

What does it mean to be a good Data Team member?

First, everyone must demonstrate active listening. As I used to explain to my high school students, this means listening with one's eyes, ears, and heart—not listening in order to respond, but listening in order to understand the person's perspective and the person's position or suggestion.

Second, all members should follow a norm that I learned years ago in a program called The Courage to Teach: presume welcome and extend welcome. This means to assume that all team members have good intentions. Even if a statement is controversial or is one with which others may disagree, if team members examine this statement by remembering that the person is most likely offering it with honorable intentions, then the resulting conversation is more likely to be productive.

Third, team members must reflect on their own practice openly, and in doing so share their successes, struggles, and ideas. Keeping potentially valuable information to oneself is not in the best interest of the team. It is often difficult to examine one's teaching objectively, and even more difficult to share one's insights with others, but this kind of openness is necessary in order for teams to function at high levels.

Last, members should adhere to the logistical rules of the meetings, which include being on time and having all needed materials ready. These materials include student work that was scored prior to the meeting.

Another role that is essential in the Data Team meeting process is the recorder. Every meeting held, whether it is a meeting during which the five steps are followed or whether it is a monitoring meeting during which the crucial sixth step occurs, must be documented through minutes or notes.

Often one member of a Data Team will fulfill the role of data technician or data coordinator. Usually this is a person who is adept at entering data and creating printouts that show the rest of the team how students are doing. Some data technicians use an Excel spreadsheet and create graphs for the team to examine at the beginning of each meeting. Others use whatever school performance-tracking software is available.

Some teams create a focus monitor role. The person serving in this role keeps the conversation focused on the meeting steps and other directly relevant issues.

A timekeeper may be used, too, and sometimes this is a dual role with the focus monitor. The timekeeper helps the facilitator put time limits to the agenda so that the team stays on topic and doesn't arrive at the end of the meeting not having gone through all the meeting steps.

A data wall curator or data display manager is another role that might be created. This person is sometimes the same person as the data technician, but that is not required. The data wall curator is responsible for displaying the team's data in whatever manner they have been directed to or as agreed upon by the team so that both teachers and students frequently see it. The displays serve as communication tools and as visible reminders of the important work of learning that all are engaged in.

Data Teams as Part of a Collaborative School Culture

Richard DuFour (2010) has said that collaborative teams are the fundamental building blocks of any learning organization and that they are "the best structure for achieving challenging goals" (p. 15). Data Teams are a vehicle that marries collaboration with classroom-based action research, and are thus an excellent model for all schools to use to meet their student achievement goals. When all Data Teams in a building have moved to the performing stage of Tuckman's model, results are truly astounding. These are the schools like those described in the next chapter where shared inquiry is an integral part of a continuous improvement process.

An inquiry orientation is important in order for Data Teams to thrive. Teams must move beyond the forming and storming stages and embrace a shared inquiry orientation. Administrators are key in establishing and nurturing this culture, but everyone in the building plays a very important role.

Initially, some teachers are hesitant to embrace the Data Teams process because they feel some type of penalty may result if the team fails to meet its goals. Also, teachers are sometimes reluctant to try new instructional practices for fear that the practices won't work well and that student learning will suffer. It is imperative that every adult involved with Data Teams implementation help create a culture where risk-taking in the name of improving student achievement is not only okay, it is celebrated.

Conclusion

Like many organizational teams, Data Teams may not operate at peak performance when initiated. However, with significant time allotted for Data Teams to meet and collaborate, and with support from administrators, these teams can become high performing and impact student achievement tremendously. Keeping an inquiry mindset and an action-research orientation is important for all educators involved in the Data Teams process. Data Team members should not be discouraged if they encounter problematic situations along the way to peak performance, as these situations are part of the natural learning journey of the team.

CHAPTER 6

Hitting Our Stride—
What High-Performing
Data Teams Do

Unlike most other chapters in this book, this chapter is not written in a question-answer format. Instead, this chapter highlights several systems and schools that cite Data Teams as being instrumental in dramatically increasing academic achievement for all students.

The essential question then becomes, "What can we learn about the effective implementation of Data Teams from these stories?" A secondary question might be, "How can my school or system adapt some of the actions of these successful sites so that we create a unique yet effective implementation plan of our own?"

System Success:
Fort Bend Independent School District (Texas)
and Lake Villa School District 41 (Illinois)

Fort Bend Independent School District (FBISD) in Sugar Land, Texas, is a large, urban system, and Lake Villa School District 41 in Illinois is a small, suburban system. However, the similarities in how these two organizations implemented Data Teams can teach us many lessons about how to begin and sustain the work of Data Teams.

Olwen Herron, Chief Accountability and Organizational Development Officer for FBISD, says that Data Teams are the vehicle that provides focus and drives the change process for the 70,000-student school district (Anderson, 2010, p. 105). Change is indeed on a monumental scale in FBISD. Fort Bend is the seventh largest school system in Texas and is incredibly diverse. It educates students who have more than 90 different home dialects and languages.

Beginning in the 2006/07 school year, FBISD partnered with The Leadership and Learning Center to create and implement a comprehensive accountability plan with the long-term goal of preparing educators to meet the needs of all Fort Bend students.

After several years of implementing the accountability plan's strategies, which include Data Teams, the district now meets or outperforms the state average at *every* grade level for *every* subject tested on the state's standardized tests. In 2009, *all* campuses met Adequate Yearly Progress (AYP), and 65 percent of the system's schools were recognized by the state of Texas for their high achievement (Anderson, 2010, p. 106).

FBISD has also made remarkable progress in closing racial and socioeconomic achievement gaps. Economically disadvantaged students, in addition to African American and Latino students, have experienced double-digit gains in performance in mathematics (Anderson, 2010, p. 106). These three groups have also made steady gains in science achievement as measured by the Texas state tests (Anderson, 2010, p. 106). At a time in education when the achievement of these particular subgroups is in the spotlight, and when the math and science performance of American students is routinely bemoaned in the media, these particular accomplishments are noteworthy. Not many systems in the United States can claim, as FBISD can, dramatic gains such as these.

FBISD began their Data Teams work with 25 targeted schools. The services provided to these schools included professional development workshops, customized on-site support from Center consultants, modeling, and coaching. Grade-level Data Teams were formed and began working to monitor student achievement by using common assessments aligned with the newly revised curriculum. Leadership teams from each school received extensive training from The Center that enabled them to teach their peers and guide the future work of the Data Teams on their campuses.

After the pilot project with the 25 neediest schools, FBISD moved to full-scale implementation of Data Teams, establishing them in every school during the following year. Support for building administrators ensured that they could facilitate the work of the teams in each building. Central office administrators and instructional area lead teachers are also very active in monitoring and supporting the work of Data Teams in buildings across the entire system.

The work of Data Teams continues to this day and produces steady gains. Another positive note: when surveyed, 70 percent of FBISD teachers said that Data Teams have had a moderate or high impact on their instructional practices (Anderson, 2010, p. 121).

In contrast with sprawling, PK–12 Fort Bend, Lake Villa School District 41 in northeast Illinois is a suburban system serving 3,300 students in grades kindergarten through 8 only. The district consists mainly of nonminority, middle-income households but is experiencing a demographic and socioeconomic shift like many other communities in the United States.

When new superintendent John Van Pelt came to the system in 2006, he convened a task force that later created a system accountability plan. This plan then guided the crafting of individual school improvement plans—creating a tight alignment of goals that did not exist before.

Along with efforts to develop aligned curriculum and assessments, Van Pelt instituted the district's form of Data Teams, called "learning teams." He calls the formation of these teams "the most ... essential professional development initiative the district has ever undertaken" (Anderson, 2010, p. 41).

The Lake Villa learning teams meet weekly and also participate in professional development designed to help them become more effective at collaborating, instructing, and assessing. The superintendent, an assistant superintendent, and principals meet with Data Teams throughout the year to monitor their effectiveness and support their ongoing work. The district also has two educators who have been trained by Center consultants to teach Data Teams to all new hires and to support the work of teams already in place.

The learning teams in Lake Villa schools take a variety of forms. In elementary schools, the teams are formed by grade level. In middle schools, the teams are formed by grade level and subject (for example, the seventh-grade language arts teachers are a team). Special education teachers, English language learning specialists, and reading resource teachers meet regularly with the various learning teams in their buildings. Special-area teachers, like those who teach physical education, music, art, and technology, have their own district-wide teams.

Lake Villa students have made consistent and significant gains on the Illinois State Achievement Test (ISAT) since 2006. The gains have been most notable in writing, going from a student proficiency level of 50 percent to the current level of 72 percent. The district has been heavily focused on literacy and has emphasized nonfiction writing across the curriculum. Van Pelt feels this emphasis has also helped boost ISAT scores in science and reading (Anderson, 2010, p. 47).

Olwen Herron calls Data Teams the vehicle that drives improvement in Fort Bend; likewise, John Van Pelt says that Data Teams have been the "cornerstone of nearly every district initiative" in Lake Villa (Anderson, 2010, p. 50). If these two dynamic educational leaders endorse Data Teams as they do, we can certainly learn from their experiences and from the admirable successes their systems have achieved.

First, a clear mission that encompasses the work of Data Teams must guide the organization. In both cases, a compelling argument was made from the very top that all children can learn at high levels and that the system can attain that goal through improved teaching. That kind of argument then served as the basis for the crafting of accountability plans. The focus of each accountability plan was squarely on student learning—and to achieve success, educators within each system knew that old ways of teaching and learning would no longer be sufficient. Effective collaboration would be necessary to improve instruction on a grand scale. Enter the Data Teams model.

Second, the success of Data Teams is heavily dependent on active, frequent, thoughtful participation of administrators at all levels. Building administrators constantly monitor the work of Data Teams by sitting in on team meetings, reviewing the minutes of those meetings, observing the agreed-upon instructional strategies in use in classrooms, debriefing with team leaders, and aligning professional development with needs that arise. Central office administrators and other instructional support personnel in turn monitor and support the work of the building administrators by supporting them in their important monitoring tasks and by providing professional development targeted to their needs. In these two systems, Data Teams aren't just something that teachers "do" and report on to their supervisors via minutes taken at the meeting. Instead, administrators are highly engaged in the work of the teams. They partner with the teachers by showing up at the meetings and in other ways.

Third, in each system, Data Teams were presented as a necessary part of ongoing improvement efforts in curriculum, instruction, and assessment. As educators revised curriculum documents, created assessments, and designed instructional units and lessons, it became necessary for them to ask themselves, "Are the students doing better? How do we know? What's the evidence?" The Data Teams model is, at its core, a collaborative, action-research model that is about much more than examining numbers. In Data Teams, teachers examine student work to determine what assistance students need in order to learn more and perform better. The best written curriculum in the land can't tell a teacher whether or not the students have grasped the most recent concepts taught—only classroom-based, real-time data in the form of student work can. In Fort Bend and Lake Villa, the process of updating the curricula necessitated that a checking mechanism be put into place, and that mechanism was Data Teams. It was not an add-on or some kind of initiative seen as "separate" from the core work of teaching. The implementation of Data Teams was an integral part of the larger school and system improvement effort.

Fourth—and related to the third lesson gleaned from these systems—teachers had time to implement Data Teams well. In the case of Fort Bend, a group of 25 pilot schools were the first to implement the process, and then other schools came on board later. In both systems, initial training in Data Teams was provided to all staff before Data Teams became a reality; teachers weren't just given a mandate to which they didn't know how to comply. Also, the teams in both places did not have to operate proficiently right out of the gate. Time and various forms of support were given to individual teams so that all teams gradually became more effective.

Fifth, each system built much-needed internal capacity by certifying some of their own personnel to deliver basic Data Teams training to others. Creating a group of in-house experts and champions is important if a large organization is to sustain the work of Data Teams over a number of years—and sustaining the work so that it is embedded in the culture of each building is the only way to ensure that Data Teams indeed help every child learn at his highest level.

School Success:
Ocean View Elementary School (Norfolk, Virginia), Gilliland Middle School (Tempe, Arizona), and Rubidoux High School (Riverside, California)

Ocean View Elementary School is situated in Norfolk, Virginia, and enrolls approximately 500 students in grades PK through 5; Gilliland Middle School is situated in Tempe, Arizona, and enrolls approximately 900 students in grades 6 through 8. Both of these schools have achieved success with the Data Teams process—Ocean View, in the long term (over a period of more than five years), and Gilliland, in only two short school years.

Lauren Campsen, the principal at Ocean View, started the work of Data Teams in earnest back in 2001, compelled by the low performance of her students on state testing and by professional development about data-driven decision making that she attended. At that time, the school had a student body that was roughly 45 percent Caucasian, 47 percent African American, and 8 percent Hispanic, with two-thirds qualifying for free/reduced lunch, and with a high rate of transiency. In the first year of Data Teams implementation, however, the school's achievement did not rise dramatically. During the summer, when the school's test scores were published, Campsen had the realization that "there's collecting data, then there's using it." She and her teachers had been collecting data and making beautiful displays of it, but they were not yet fully using it to change their instructional practice.

That changed the next year. Campsen formed vertical teams in addition to the horizontal teams and appointed four subject-area specialists to assist in the efforts. When the results came back, the faculty was not disappointed a second time. The school experienced dramatic gains. Third-grade reading and math, for instance, increased by an average of 27 percentage points over the previous year.

The school was a 2008 recipient of the Blue Ribbon award and, in that year, reported impressive results. In 2008, 100 percent of Hispanic students and 99 percent of African American students followed by 94 percent of Caucasian students in grades 3 through 5 performed at proficient or advanced levels on the state exam.

This type of performance continues as this chapter is written in 2010. The racial achievement gap has effectively been eliminated.

Teachers in many middle schools across the United States would love to welcome students who, when in fifth grade, scored proficient or higher on their state tests, like the students in Campsen's school. Mastering the objectives on the state tests of previous years often allows teachers to do less reteaching and remediation.

Gilliland Middle School in Tempe, Arizona, is home to 900 students in grades 6 through 8. Administrators and teachers at the school, like many of their counterparts across the nation, were unhappy with the performance of their students on standardized tests, so they decided to take action. They were also targeted for corrective action by the state of Arizona.

Teachers at Gilliland developed their curriculum maps, used Data Teams to monitor the progress of students, and implemented several effective instructional strategies, including the increased use of nonfiction writing and a focus on academic vocabulary. In four years' time, they went from being on academic watch to meeting AYP and being a "performing plus" school in Arizona—meaning that they have made dramatic improvement in student achievement.

Data Teams do indeed work in secondary schools, as Gilliland Middle School demonstrates. High schools can also use the Data Teams model to dramatically raise student achievement. Rubidoux High School in Southern California is a glowing example of how Data Teams can make a profound impact on student learning at the high school level.

Principal Jay Trujillo vividly remembers the day he saw his school featured on the front page of the local newspaper as one of the worst in the area. Rubidoux ranked in the lowest decile when compared to similar California high schools. In Riverside County, the school was listed as number 33 of 36 high schools. As Trujillo remembers it, he understood very clearly that the school had to produce results immediately or face harsh state sanctions.

Rubidoux is a large high school, at the time made up of 2,450 students who were 61 percent Latino, 28 percent Caucasian, and 8 percent African American (with other ethnic groups composing the remainder). Almost a fifth of the school was designated as English Language Learners, and 39 percent were eligible for free/reduced lunch. Over a period of five years, however, Rubidoux became the number one improved high school in Southern California, with approximately 80 other high schools falling in line behind it. The school has set three consecutive school records for daily attendance, shattering records that were 47 years old, and has dramatically increased the number of students who say they plan to attend college (from 46 percent to 75 percent). Rubidoux has done this despite becoming more ethnically diverse and more socioeconomically challenged.

Trujillo credits his work with The Center over five years for the turnaround. The school worked on developing curriculum and assessments in addition to implementing Data Teams. Trujillo notes that the staff was very busy, but that the results certainly paid off.

What can we learn from these school success stories?

First, if you are the principal, give the call for urgency. Improved results can wait no longer. If 100 percent of students are not meeting or exceeding grade-level standards, then there is work to be done.

Second, get others to partner with you to emphasize the urgency. Teachers best sell the idea of Data Teams to other teachers. Partner with the influential teacher-leaders in your school and take action.

Third, stick to it. Don't just try Data Teams for a few months or even one school year. The work is hard but gratifying. And it will get results. Remember the moral of the fable of the tortoise and the hare: "Slow and steady wins the race." True collaboration that impacts student achievement takes time, and the time invested is worth it in the long run.

Last, don't forget to celebrate. Small wins lead to big wins. With every Data Team cycle, students are learning and teachers are growing. Administrators and teachers alike should remember to celebrate their successes and recognize students for their efforts and continuous improvement.

REFLECTION QUESTIONS

1. From a system perspective, what value, if any, do you see in beginning with "pilot" schools, like Fort Bend Independent School District did?

2. How do central-level and building-level administrators in your system currently interact with teachers to examine the effectiveness of instruction? How do you envision their roles and actions changing in order to increase the effectiveness of instruction?

3. Which teacher-leaders come to mind as you think about people who could possibly teach their peers about Data Teams and support the ongoing work?

4. Are there small victories about effective instruction and increased achievement that could be celebrated right now in your school or system? How could these be celebrated?

5. What are your next steps with forming or sustaining Data Teams?

CHAPTER 7

Under the Magnifying Glass— The Steps in More Detail

The five steps that Data Teams follow in each meeting were introduced in Chapter 3. Step Six, monitoring and evaluating results, may not be an explicit part of some Data Team meetings, but informal monitoring occurs as teams sit together and collectively reflect on their use of strategies and review student work samples at Steps Two and Four.

In this chapter, the five basic meeting steps are explained in greater detail. For each step, three levels of team performance are described: progressing (not yet meeting standard or operating proficiently), proficient, and exemplary. (Also see the Appendix for the rubric used in The Center's Data Teams Feedback Service.)

For each of the five basic meeting steps, common problems are highlighted, and possible adaptations are shared. These scenarios are derived from the work of several Center associates who have assisted both their own schools and also entire systems with Data Teams implementation, in addition to my ongoing work in Elkhart Community Schools (Indiana), Lakeland Central School District (New York), and St. Paul Public Schools (Minnesota).

Step 1: Collect and Chart Data

In Step One in a typical Data Team meeting, the team members examine pre-assessment data in preparation for the focused instruction that will come or post-assessment data to determine if the desired student learning goals were met. Charting student performance results is a first step that helps teachers to prioritize areas of concern related to student learning.

This step requires teachers to collaborate around a set of data from an assessment that all members administered to their students. The data can be sent to someone on the team prior to the meeting so that it is assembled and ready to view when the meeting begins, or the team may process and chart the data on the spot, with each person reporting in turn until all data is shared.

Prior to Step One occurring, the common assessment must have been created (ideally by the team in a collaborative fashion) and administered. Assessment design and administration are not part of the Data Team meeting; they must occur at another dedicated time.

Progressing teams who are completing Step One may spend time criticizing the assessment itself or particular items that appear on it, thus taking valuable time away from digging deeper into the students' responses. Even on assessments that are flawed in design, valuable information about student learning resides in the answers. Side issues like the quality of the assessment or details about the administration are often not appropriate for conversation at Step One, as time is usually limited, and the team must immediately move toward examining student work for what it indicates about the current state of learning.

Progressing teams may also have one or more members who do not report their data. This can occur for various reasons. The member may not have finished scoring the work when the meeting occurs. Obviously this situation must be remedied if the team is to become proficient, because without current information about the learning of all students represented by the team, the best instructional strategy remedies cannot be determined.

Other reasons for a team having incomplete data include a member who is late to or absent from the meeting. In these instances, the team should not wait. Waiting for someone or their data can force the meeting agenda to run too long, and it is absolutely vital that plenty of time be reserved for Steps Four and Five. Teams must operate with the information they have at hand, on time. As Douglas Reeves often says, "Perfection is not an option" (2002, p. 52). A Data Team must make inferences and generate hypotheses about how to raise student achievement based on the information they have, even if it is incomplete. If their strategies do not prove as effective as they had predicted, then the team can collectively determine its next steps. The team should not be paralyzed into inaction because of incomplete data. However, in the long run, teams must find ways to ensure they have both timely and complete data so that their actions become increasingly targeted to the students' most urgent learning needs.

Another indication of a progressing team is dividing student performance into only two categories at Step One: those students who have met or gone beyond the standard (proficient and higher) and those who are not yet proficient. When I first learned the Data Teams process almost a decade ago, this is where my team started, under the guidance of our Center consultant. This is a necessary beginning step for teams, but is not sufficient. Other performance levels must be delineated so that the full range of student learning is better understood. With the pressures on educators to examine subgroup performance and to react to individual student needs rapidly, simply knowing who has met the standard and who has not is no longer sufficient. However, for some teams, it can be an important fundamental step.

Proficient teams complete Step One in just a few minutes, saving precious time for the analysis of student work that comes at Step Two. They quickly and accurately chart or report the number of students that actually took the assessment. They then divide student performance into several meaningful categories (which have been predetermined). Often, these categories include the number and names of students who are proficient and higher, those who are predicted to be proficient after instructional strategies are applied, those who need targeted instruction or additional time to meet the standard, and those who require intensive interventions.

If multiple standards or objectives were covered on any given assessment, the data is ideally displayed in a form that makes it clear what the levels of student proficiency are for each standard/objective. When Data Teams first begin working, they may choose to design assessments based on only one prioritized standard or expected learning goal in order to provide both brevity and clarity. However, as teams increase in their sophistication, they often design assessments that focus on multiple prioritized standards or expected learning goals—or assessments that blend "old" items with new, effectively checking to see if previous learning has been retained.

In Step One, teachers should organize students on the chart (or other data display) using consistent, preestablished guidelines or cut points for the articulated performance levels. These guidelines or cut points should have been firmly established when the assessment was created (outside the Data Team meeting). Proficient teams do not spend time in the Data Team meeting debating what makes each performance level different from the others. This is a discussion that is fruitful at two other times (and possibly more). Those times are when the assessment is being created and in the monitoring meetings that occur between meetings at which pre- or post-assessment data is being discussed.

Finally, proficient teams translate the numbers of students in each performance level into percentages that will help the team establish one or more SMART goals in Step Three. It is important to use percentages to get a more global view of the entire group of students that the team is responsible for. Using raw numbers can be misleading or problematic in some cases because of student transiency, student absenteeism, or school events or disruptions. Focusing on the individual students in each proficiency level is helpful as a "microview," but viewing overall percentages is also helpful as a "macroview." Both views work in harmony to inform the team.

A proficient team would have a chart like the one in Exhibit 7.1 at the end of Step One. This particular team lists only the names of students who are proficient or higher and those of the ones who are already in need of intensive assistance so that the team can keep these students foremost in their minds as they determine next steps. The single standard addressed on this particular pre-assessment was about students being able to make valid inferences when reading on-grade-level informational text.

Exemplary teams not only examine the numbers and names of students who have performed in the various established levels but also disaggregate the data in relation to the school's most pressing needs. For example, an exemplary team using the data in Exhibit 7.1 could disaggregate the data for the 24 percent and 38 percent of students who appear in the two "could be proficient" groups even further. They could examine this information disaggregated by race/ethnicity, socioeconomic factors, low attendance, or other variables. This information could then be compared to the school's overall academic performance so the team can discern whether there

 EXHIBIT 7.1 **Example of Step One, Data Reporting**

Teacher Names	Number of students assessed	Number and/or names of students who are proficient and higher	Number and/or names of students who will likely be proficient after instruction	Number and/or names of students in need of targeted instruction or additional time	Number and/or names of students in need of extensive intervention
Gregg	24	4 Michelle, Katie, Andrea, Jordan	5	10	5 Jada, Eileen, Tomas, Deke, Isaiah
Lassiter	20	0	5	5	10 Linda, Juan, Tracey, Mike, Cathy, Doug, Larry, Cecilia, Paul, Jillian
Cordova	28	3 Austin, Carla, Cedric	7	13	5 Tony, Laura, Emily, Howie, Jake
Total	72	10%	24%	38%	28%

are common patterns of low performance, whether there are areas of high achievement that can be celebrated, and whether there are important anomalies that the team can investigate further.

Another benefit to deeper data analysis via disaggregation is that additional school-based academic services may be identified for students in all the nonproficient categories. Obviously, the team's primary goal is to make changes in their own instructional practice as a result of better understanding the learning needs of their students—but if they are able to secure additional, out-of-classroom assistance for nonproficient students, this kind of support can work very well in tandem with improved core instruction.

Step 2: Analyze Data and Prioritize Needs

In Step Two, a Data Team analyzes student work from the common assessment in order to identify the strengths students display in their learning in addition to their most urgent learning needs. Their most urgent learning needs become the focus for future changes in instruction.

Another benefit of Step Two is that successful instructional strategies can be identified for celebration and, ideally, for replication. When student work samples are examined closely, even subtle differences in performance can teach educators a great deal, not only about the students but about the teaching behind the performance.

Progressing teams often spend time at Step Two simply labeling what is "right" and "wrong" instead of digging deeper into the student work to find out why answers are correct or not. They also frequently cite learning challenges that are beyond a teacher's direct control, such as the following:

- The student didn't learn the concept or skill in the previous grade level or course.
- The student doesn't do his homework.
- The student is often tardy or absent.
- The student's home situation prevents him from doing well at school.

Progressing teams often struggle with prioritizing students' learning needs. They may end up with more than three academic needs that all seem equally pressing. Thus, they are unable to enter the discussion of instructional strategies with a clear focus or simply become overwhelmed because all the needs seem equally important. Often when progressing teams feel overwhelmed, they reach Step Three and are not able to articulate a SMART goal that zooms in clearly enough on a learning target. For example, in Step Two a team may discover that students are weak in solving equations that have one variable. Since this is a multistep process, the team must seek answers to the following by examining the student work:

- Do students understand what a variable represents? Where is the evidence that supports our answer?
- When students isolate the variable, do they remember to do an equivalent operation to the other side of the equation? How often do students forget to do this?
- Do students simply make copying mistakes when isolating the variable and "bringing it down"?
- Do students label their answer when necessary? If not, why not?

The determination of strategies to employ that occurs in Step Four of the meeting depends on teams answering questions like those posed above. Simple copying errors would be addressed quite differently in mathematics instruction than would not doing equivalent operations to both sides of the equation.

Proficient teams focus on student needs that are directly within teachers' control. They do not spend time discussing issues that they cannot directly influence through their instructional strategies, like a student's discipline problems or family matters.

These teams search for the root causes of students' incorrect responses and also look deeply into students' correct answers for clues about how to take them to even higher performance levels. They reference targeted prioritized standards or learning goals as they examine student work, ensuring that the students have been accurate and thorough in their answers.

When discussing student needs, proficient teams prioritize in order to be most strategic or to get the "biggest bang for the buck" in instruction. To continue with the example provided earlier, understanding what a variable represents and remembering to perform equivalent operations on each side of an equation are far more important conceptually than not bringing a term down correctly or not labeling one's final answer. A proficient team might state the goal in Step Three by saying students will be proficient in solving equations accurately, but their strategies might specifically address the prioritized need of understanding the "golden rule of algebra"—whatever you do to one side of an equation, you must also do to the other side.

Proficient teams categorize students into several levels of performance and might prioritize needs differently for each group—depending, of course, on what they find in the student work. Sometimes students who are close to proficiency and those who are a little further away have similar confusions, inaccuracies, or limited understandings. All the actions the team decides to take must be rooted in the close examination of student work.

The minutes of one proficient team, in Exhibit 7.2, reflect effective discussion of what the students who are close to reaching proficiency know and can do. This excerpt also reflects numerous valid inferences made from the close examination of student work. (The assessment task was for students to write an accurate summary paragraph after reading a short, on-grade-level informational text.)

EXHIBIT 7.2	Example of Step Two, Analyzing Student Work

Notes about Student Performance	Our Inferences
Strengths: *What do proficient students know, and what can they do proficiently?* • They were able to determine what was important • They pulled specific content from question • They used specific examples or supporting details (at least three) • Mechanics like spelling were not distracting • They used transitions between sentences	• They know to base their answer specifically on the question that has been posed • They have been taught about organization of a paragraph: topic sentence, several details, conclusion sentence • Students who are proficient readers and write like real writers, use correct mechanics and transitions to move the reader along
Challenges: *What do students struggle with, misunderstand, or need help with?* • They included everything from the original text vs. focusing on the most important details • Their sense of sentence structure or variety was weak; many sentences start the same way or are structured alike • Their sense of mechanics is below grade level, especially in punctuation • Their summary was written in a structure more like a think-aloud than in any certain order	• They might not know what "summary" means—that it focuses only on important information • They are not sure how to determine importance of details and to weed out those that don't need to be in a summary • They need help in structuring and punctuating various types of sentences correctly

Prioritized Needs:
- Students need to know what "summary" means and see models of proficient summary paragraphs.
- Students need to understand sentence and paragraph structure better.

Exemplary teams take their analysis at Step Two even further, prioritizing the students' learning needs in order to reflect areas that not only impact the standard or topic at hand, but also have a large impact across standards, topics, and even disciplines. In the example already shared, this might mean discussing terms like *equal, equation, equivalence, variable,* and *balance* in a broader context, helping students connect these terms to other disciplines. Numerous researchers (Allen, 1999; Graves, 2005; Marzano, 2004) have documented that a focus on academic vocabulary benefits students in math class and beyond, so a team that would integrate this focus would be impacting much more than just the students' understanding of equations.

Exemplary teams, like proficient teams, determine urgent needs for the various groups of students based on what they see in the work itself. However, exemplary teams are particularly expert in prioritizing the needs for the group of students that requires intensive intervention. The teachers spend time figuring out what this particular group of students is lacking as far as prerequisite skills and knowledge as they search for root causes. They then create a hierarchy of needs so that all assistance given to the identified students is focused on what will help the students the most, the soonest. In other words, they think more in terms of *acceleration* rather than remediation—which is critical for this group of students because they often are deficient in many skills and lack important conceptual knowledge. If the most important learning needs aren't addressed fast and well for these students, they continue to slip behind.

Step 3: Set, Review, or
Revise Incremental SMART Goals

Step Three is all about setting a short-term goal that can be reached in a brief instructional cycle (generally one week to one month). Working toward one or more SMART goals helps focus a team so that their analysis of what students need turns into measurable adult actions. The goal-setting step promotes team accountability and commitment to improved student learning.

When setting, reviewing, or revising a goal in Step Three, Data Teams should revisit the percentages arrived at in Step One. The students who are close to proficiency (likely to be proficient after focused instruction) and those who are further away but not in need of intensive intervention should all be considered when setting the SMART goal.

Some teams prefer to take a "safe" route and simply calculate what the total percentage of proficient students would be if every student from the "close to proficient" category moved to proficient at the end of the instruction cycle. This is an acceptable path. Other teams, however, consider "close to proficient" students in addition to some or all students in the next category down. Some teams even prefer to take a bold route and set a very high goal because they feel the targeted learning is important enough to have all students (or as close to all as possible) proficient in it. These teams often set goals to have 80 percent or more of their students reaching proficiency. While an 80 percent proficiency level might seem daunting at first, remember that if the team falls short of the goal, the team has the authority to act in response.

Any SMART goal, by definition, contains five parts, as follows:

- Specific

- Measurable

- Achievable

- Relevant

- Timely

Here is an example of a correctly written SMART goal: The percentage of <u>fifth-grade students</u> proficient and higher in <u>writing a summary paragraph based on the reading of a short informational text</u> will increase from <u>39 percent</u> to <u>50 percent</u> as measured by a <u>short constructed-response item on the unit test</u>, which will be administered on <u>September 10 or 11</u>.

Progressing teams often do not write SMART goals; however, they generally write general goals that do help them focus their work. Often they do not set the percentage of proficient students that they want to meet the goals and instead say or write things like, "Fourth-grade students will improve in long division" or "Sophomores will write better persuasive essays." These goals are too vague to qualify as SMART goals.

Another area in which progressing teams can improve is in the timeliness of the goal. These teams sometimes allow the window of time for administering the state's standardized tests to serve as the end part of their goal statements. This is detrimental to the team's progress. Teams must set short-cycle goals so that they can monitor students' progress incrementally and make adjustments to instruction as needed.

Progressing teams also sometimes move on to a new goal even if post-assessment data indicates that additional instruction might be needed. This occurs most often when teams set low goals, such as moving from 2 percent of students proficient on a pre-assessment to 33 percent on a post-assessment. If the goal is for 33 percent, or roughly one-third, of students to reach proficiency, this means that *two-thirds of students* could have significant learning needs in relation to the targeted skills and concepts, but the goal was still met. Does the team move on to other learning targets if only 33 percent of students are proficient in the ones previously identified? In most cases, the targeted learning should continue to be addressed through instructional strategies, including the use of differentiation.

Progressing teams sometimes make decisions based on incomplete information or emotions. They also sometimes get sidetracked by "outliers"—those particular questions or answers on an assessment that are wildly different from most others. For example, if there is one poorly worded question on an assessment, and the team did not catch the problem before the assessment was administered, almost all students could have answered it incorrectly. While this situation is interesting, it is not worthy of lengthy discussion in the Data Team meeting. The item could be disregarded entirely in the calculation of proficiency rates in order to diminish its impact, and the meeting could proceed. However, if team members spend too much time analyzing a flawed item, they steal precious time from analyzing other aspects of student work that could be far more illustrative.

Proficient teams consistently create complete SMART goals that guide their work. Whether or not they meet their goal in any given instructional cycle is less important than what they do in response to the results. They do not get discouraged when they fall short of a goal but immediately make plans for what they should do next to meet it or surpass it.

Exemplary teams differ from proficient teams in that they consistently target needs that reach across disciplines, such as writing an accurate summary or stating and justifying predictions. They may also set separate SMART goals for those students who will experience intensive intervention. These goals are clearly linked to the prerequisite skills and knowledge that the students are lacking or are severely deficient in. These goals may then be used not only in the team members' classrooms but also as progress-monitoring tools for other adults in the building who work with those students.

Step 4: Select Common Instructional Strategies

In Step Four, Data Team members must consider the prioritized learning needs of their students as they determine the actions they will take. In order for this step to be productive, they must discuss specific, research-based instructional strategies that they feel will have immediate impact on student learning. It is this step of the Data Teams protocol that changes practice.

Instructional strategies are the actions of the teacher that increase cognition in relation to an identified learning goal (Leadership and Learning Center, 2009). Strategies are not activities like "Complete a set of practice problems for homework." That statement is not a strategy because it tells what the *student* will do, not what the *teacher* will do. Strategies are also not agenda items or class activities like a math "warm-up" or "bell ringer." Strategies are written from the point of view of the adults who will be responsible for using them, and descriptions of strategies must get directly at the thinking (cognition) required.

Progressing teams may display a limited knowledge of research-based strategies or agree on activities and assignments versus strategies. They may spend time discussing learning-environment strategies like "Create a word wall" or organizational strategies like "Increase parent involvement by having more open houses." These strategy statements do not indicate the cognition that must be executed by students in order to attain the desired learning goal.

Progressing teams also sometimes discuss strategies that are only loosely related to the learning goals. For example, if the learning target (and SMART goal) indicates that students will be proficient in writing summary paragraphs, the strategy of asking students to set personalized goals for summary writing would probably not be as effective as teaching students to use a graphic organizer that helps them plan their summaries.

Proficient teams analyze each possible or suggested strategy in terms of impact on student learning. They are able to tightly "fit" research-based strategies to student needs and spend time discussing how the strategies can be carried out with fidelity. This means that they take time at Step Four to discuss how each of them will enact the strategy, including the teachers' specific actions and the time spent on those actions.

Proficient teams select only strategies for which they themselves will be held accountable both by the team and by building leadership. This means that there will be explicit evidence of each person's use of the agreed-upon strategies. They continuously seek to refine and strengthen these practices so the practices can be applied to future situations and, in some cases, for replication throughout the building.

Exemplary teams choose strategies that have broad impact—across subjects, across grade levels, and in many areas of a student's academic life. One such strategy is teaching students to use Cornell notes, a form of note-taking that has been correlated with higher achievement in science (Reeves, 2008, p. 14). If a science Data Team were to enact the frequent use of Cornell notes in their classes, students would then be able to access a tool to increase their learning not only in science but in all situations where teachers might ask them to take notes.

Exemplary teams also study effective strategies with each other, during team meetings as time allows, and outside of team meetings as part of their own professional growth. They ensure every team member knows how to implement the agreed-upon strategies, using modeling during the meeting if necessary. These teams are also often called upon by administrators to share their successful practices with other teachers so that replication of success unfolds.

Step 5: Determine Results Indicators

The final step in a Data Team meeting is determining results indicators, which may be both quantitative and qualitative. This step helps teachers to monitor progress toward the SMART goal(s) and to gauge the success of the instructional strategies.

At their core, results indicators are "if, then" statements. In short, if teachers implement this *strategy*, then students and teachers see these *results indicators*. Results indicators are critical in order to monitor the adult actions and to make clear their accountability, in addition to articulating the evidence that is seen once the adult actions occur.

Results indicators help teams see how cause data and effect data are linked. In a Data Teams context, *effect data* is information about student performance gathered from assessment tasks, including standardized tests. Effect data captures an end result. Effect data can also consist of "look fors" that are present in student work; for example, students are able to write effective conclusions in essays or are able to explain their mathematics reasoning when solving multistep problems.

Cause data, on the other hand, is information about what is happening that leads to a particular result. In a Data Teams context, cause data is information about what the teachers do to increase student learning—it is information about their instructional strategies. So, if more students than ever are able to write effective conclusions in essays or explain their mathematics reasoning when solving multistep problems, what did the adults do to get them there? The actions that the adults took to help the students become more proficient are the heart of the cause data.

Progressing teams state student achievement results when they are asked to write their results indicators. So they may record something like the following in their meeting minutes: "Most students will be able to produce an effective summary paragraph when asked to do so." While this is a results indicator, there are several more that such a team could cite, like the following, taken from the work of a real Data Team in New York:

- Students display conceptual knowledge of summarizing when participating in class discussions, using words such as *concise, deletion,* and *substitution.*

- Teachers of all subjects are requiring students to write at least one summary per week, focused on the content of the class.

- In science classes, students are becoming increasingly adept at writing the summary portion of Cornell notes.

Progressing teams may have difficulty examining student learning based on assessment scores rather than on observation. They also struggle with describing the explicit teacher actions that indicate the teacher is implementing the agreed-upon instructional strategies with fidelity. So they may say a results indicator is, "The graphic organizer that the team agreed on is posted on each teacher's wall." A more specific results indicator statement would be, "Each teacher models the use of the graphic organizer daily during either reading or writing workshop time." The best results indicators are highly specific and link directly to a human action, whether it is the adult action that led to a change in learning or the student action that proves increased proficiency.

Proficient teams describe, as specifically as possible, the teacher actions that can be seen when the selected instructional strategies are implemented. They are also adept at stating the student actions that provide evidence that the strategies have been implemented. To continue with the example presented in the last paragraph, a student-oriented results indicator might be, "Students are observed using the graphic organizer they were taught not only during the language arts block but also during social studies and science instruction."

Proficient teams frequently describe the change in student performance in their results indicators in a way that differs from merely stating the percentage of proficiency reflected in the team's SMART goal. For example, instead of a results indicator being, "85 percent of students can write a summary paragraph meeting the 3 level on the state rubric," it might be, "Students start their summaries with topic sentences that are focused on the most important features of the information."

Exemplary teams go beyond the work of proficient teams by establishing interim "check-in" times to monitor the implementation of the strategies, rather than waiting for the next meeting at which there is fresh assessment information available. These teams also write clear, detailed descriptions of their results indicators so that other teachers can replicate the strategies. Clear, detailed results indicators written into the minutes also help administrators look for the strategies in use as they drop in and out of classrooms. Last, exemplary teams write results indicators that help them accurately predict student performance on the next assessment. These teams are envisioning the successful application of instructional strategies as displayed in future student work.

Conclusion

The five steps that Data Teams follow in most meetings are crucial to the smooth functioning of the teams and lead to vastly improved student learning when applied well. While it may take considerable time for some Data Teams to reach a proficient performance level at each step, other teams move to proficient or exemplary performance quickly. Regardless of the level of performance at any given step, however, Data Teams can continuously monitor and evaluate their own work via Step Six and personal reflection. In this way, Data Teams work is constantly refined and improved, and students are the greatest beneficiaries.

CHAPTER 8

Troubleshooting and Frequently Asked Questions

This chapter addresses common questions about Data Teams. The questions and answers are grouped topically as follows:

Questions about the Formation and Composition of Teams

Questions about the Logistics of Data Team Meetings

Questions about Interactions among Team Members

Questions about Instructional Strategies

Questions about Assessments

Questions about the Formation and Composition of Teams

1. How large should a team be? What number is "too big"?

The largest team I have ever personally worked with consisted of 10 members. This was an interdisciplinary, middle school team comprised of two teachers of each core subject (math, English, social studies, science) along with a special education teacher and an electives teacher. While this is one of the largest teams that my colleagues and I have ever worked with, it was a highly effective team. The team operated under a charge from the building leaders that everyone use nonfiction writing across the curriculum, so the main objective was clear from the start. The Data Team leader was competent and ensured clear communication and smooth, time-efficient meetings. The meetings were held weekly and lasted for one hour during a common prep period. Every meeting had an appointed timekeeper and note taker, and the notes were e-mailed to the entire team the morning after the meeting.

Some elementary principals with whom I've consulted feel that a team larger than five members is too large, and in at least two elementary schools I'm aware of, the principals have split a grade-level team into two teams based on this concern. *However, this configuration is not recommended by The Center.* Keeping all educators who share the same grade level together as a team is recommended if at all possible so that the most important learning targets for that grade level are monitored collectively.

The bottom line is that it's not the size of the team that is important—it's the effectiveness of the team. If a team can conduct frequent meetings and consistently enact all six steps of the Data Teams process for results, then that is far more important than the size of the team.

2. Which is best at the middle school level, interdisciplinary or subject-area teams?

My colleagues and I have worked with effective teams of both types. If there is a school-wide focus or directive upon which the interdisciplinary teams focus, they can be highly effective. For example, some middle schools that have worked with The Center have focused on nonfiction writing across the curriculum. Interdisciplinary teams with such a focus can give a periodic, common writing prompt and monitor the students' progress based on the scoring rubric. Then, in the teachers' individual classes, various writing strategies can be employed to provide students with additional practice and feedback. Cross-curricular writing strategies can also be used in the individual classes. In this way, the Data Team monitors writing by using the monthly or bimonthly writing-on-demand tasks, and each teacher then follows up with the common instructional strategies *plus additional writing practice* within his class.

A focus on reading for information or problem solving can also be implemented school-wide in a similar fashion.

Other possible configurations at the middle school level include two or more teachers of the same exact course being on a team together (for example, three eighth-grade English language arts teachers), or vertical teams of the same subject (for example, six math teachers, two each from the sixth, seventh, and eighth grades). A vertical team must focus on an important learning target that impacts each grade, for example writing persuasive essays, reading informational text in the content area, or solving open-ended math problems that use more than one mathematical operation.

3. High school teachers have multiple preparations. On how many teams should a high school teacher serve?

When starting Data Teams at the high school level, it is critical to assign each teacher to only one team. Even though most high school teachers have two subject preparations or more, there will be only enough time in most Data Team meeting schedules for each teacher to work with one team. Also, it is impractical and very time consuming for high school teachers, most of whom teach 75 to 150 students each day, to participate in the designing of and collaborative scoring of common assessments while also fully engaging in multiple Data Team meetings. In some systems, this amount of work would also violate the teacher's contract.

Some large middle and high schools begin Data Teams work with a "pilot" class for each teacher. So, for example, if a teacher were teaching three sections of ninth-grade English and one of tenth-grade English (as I did for many years), the pilot class might be the first-period English class. That means each teacher on this particular teacher's Data Team would report scores from only the pilot class during Data Team meetings and would bring only those work samples to the meetings.

This concession of working with only a pilot class instead of using the Data Teams process with all of one's classes is usually made by an administrator who is experiencing push-back from teachers with 100 or more students, or in the case of system contractual limitations. And while this type of pilot program is not endorsed by The Center, what invariably happens is just what the administrators suspected from the outset—the best teachers quickly conduct the Data Team assessments and employ the agreed-upon instructional strategies in *all of the classes* of that particular preparation.

If an administrator is going to go for full implementation and not the piloting scenario described above, then each teacher should be assigned to a Data Team for a particular course. The administrator must consider the number of class periods that teachers teach each course and also the makeup of every team. The teacher who spends 75 percent of his time teaching ninth-grade English and only 25 percent teaching tenth-grade English might be a good candidate for the tenth-grade Data Team if he brings unique qualities to the team or could be a strong Data Team leader. The number of times a teacher teaches any given class does not necessarily correlate directly with the teacher's Data Team assignment.

4. What about singletons and electives?

Small schools and schools that offer advanced or specialized course work have handled this situation in various ways.

One solution is to have teachers of singleton courses come together and find a common focus within the framework of goals that have been articulated in the school improvement plan or in support of an initiative the principal has established. For example, a physical education and health team at the high school level could establish a focus on reading informational text, or a team of "specials" teachers at the elementary level (music, art, physical education, etc.) could form and support an overall school focus on writing or problem solving. These teachers of diverse subjects would then work together to assess the specified focus skills as these skills directly impact learning in their classes.

In some systems, teachers of the same course or discipline come together once a month or on dedicated in-service days and work in a modified Data Teams process. For example, if a school system has only three music teachers who share all the elementary schools, these teachers can meet and can have common assessments based on their own content or in support of other system initiatives, like using writing across the curriculum.

In other systems, especially at the high school level, teachers of very specialized subjects can come together on in-service days or by using technology to hold meetings via videoconference or webinar. They can also continue their conversations via e-mail or message board. For example, perhaps there are only two teachers of physics in a large, rural school system, and the school system holds only two days of system-wide in-service a year, one in the fall and another in the spring. These two teachers could develop common assessments and share with each other via e-mail, message board, Internet videoconferencing, and so on.

In rare instances, such as in rural schools where many teachers teach multiple singleton courses, the Data Teams process must be modified to meet each site's unique needs. In some cases, the teacher of a singleton course may individually go through the steps of pre-assessment, analysis, goal-setting, instructional adjustments, and post-assessment, and then meet with another teacher or administrator to discuss the process and to share insights. In other cases, the entire faculty may go through such a process individually and then convene in small groups to share their findings.

5. Should a coach or administrator ever be a Data Team leader?

Data Teams are intended to impact instruction at the teacher-student level and thus should be directed by teachers. However, in some extreme cases of team dysfunction, administrators have "taken over" Data Team meetings for the short term, and for the short term only.

It is not recommended that administrators or instructional coaches assume the position of Data Team leader for more than a few data cycles. However, instructional coaches can serve as useful ad hoc members for many Data Teams—they can sit in on meetings as a regular duty or as invited in order to share ideas about instructional strategies.

It is important to remember that the building leaders must monitor and support Data Teams in order for them to be effective. So, it follows that the principal must do whatever he feels that it takes in order to get Data Teams up and running and to make them increasingly effective over time.

Questions about the Logistics of Data Team Meetings

1. How much time is required for a meeting?

From the very beginnings of Data Teams work, Center associates have always recommended at least one hour for a Data Team meeting; however, we do recognize that in many schools and systems, this amount of time may not be available.

It is particularly difficult, especially in the early stages of Data Teams work, to conduct a meeting that includes serious attention to all five basic steps in less than an hour, much less to attend to monitoring and evaluating. Time constraints have sometimes prevented teams from determining instructional strategies because they did not get to Step Four. If teams don't have time for Step Four, then they are missing the true essence of the meeting: to change instruction immediately in response to student learning needs.

If your team has less than an hour available to meet, consider reserving at least 10 minutes for Steps Two and Four, the analysis of student work and the selection of common instructional strategies. If less than one hour is available, the assessment data should also be submitted to the Data Team leader or data technician beforehand to reduce the time spent on Step One.

Regardless of the time recommendations that Center personnel might give to schools, the most important consideration is that a Data Team at least get through the basic five steps in every meeting. Some highly efficient Data Teams are able to move through the five meeting steps in approximately 40 minutes, but they have achieved this level of efficiency only after considerable practice.

2. How often should teams meet?

A decade ago, when The Center's associates were still in the early stages of promoting and teaching the concept of Data Teams, the recommendation for a minimum number of meetings was once a month. However, since that time we have discovered that the teams who meet most frequently are the teams that experience the most success.

Data Teams should meet and go through the five-step process at least every two weeks. If this frequency is not attainable, a school or system should strive to be as close to the recommendation as possible.

Between the meetings in which new achievement data is examined, monitoring meetings should occur. So in the ideal cycle where a team meets every two weeks to examine data, there are also meetings in the "off" weeks. These meetings are used for the members to make midcourse corrections, celebrate results, and continually reflect on their practice (Leadership and Learning Center, 2010).

Team members must also keep in mind that other times should be reserved for the development of common formative assessments.

Questions about Interactions among Team Members

1. How important is the Data Team leader? What qualities must this person have in order to run the meetings well?

A good Data Team leader is a teacher-leader within his building. This person commands the respect of his peers and is known as an effective teacher and a lifelong learner—probably a person who reads professionally, attends conferences, and can influence others to change their practices.

Good grade-level or department chairs sometimes make good Data Team leaders, and sometimes not. Just because a person is a good manager or very detail oriented does not mean that person will be able to lead a Data Team effectively.

An effective Data Team leader must be both a good listener and a good questioner. The most articulate and vocal faculty member is not necessarily the best choice. The Data Team leader must be able to get others to listen and to contribute. He must also walk the fine line between teacher-leader and administrator. Because a Data Team leader does not serve in any supervisory capacity but does take a leadership role, he must make it clear to teammates that everyone on the team is equal. The leader does not judge the effectiveness of any other teacher or coerce other teachers to do things his way.

In some cases, schools have Data Teams with co-leaders, or Data Team leader positions that rotate after a certain amount of time. Administrators must consider a number of factors when determining who their Data Team leaders will be, so there is not one "right" way to select Data Team leaders for any one system or building.

2. What if one person tries to dominate the conversation?

Many teams have the one member who wants to dominate the conversation, whether that person goes off on tangents or wants to discuss side issues or wants to dictate the instructional strategies himself. In some cases, this person wants to create all the assessments, timelines, and class activities.

A Data Team is a collaborative group. No one member should dominate. If the dominant member is the Data Team leader, it is incumbent upon the other members to either speak up or to seek help from an instructional coach or administrator.

In the cases in which the dominant member is not the leader, then the leader should attempt to minimize the contributions of that person and to invite increased participation from others.

The timekeeper and focus monitor can also help in this kind of situation. For example, if the timekeeper says something like, "We have now spent five minutes discussing Mrs. Jones' views on the assessment. Can we return to a discussion of the five steps? We were analyzing student work, Step Two," then the team gets the message that it's time to minimize Mrs. Jones' comments and get back to work.

3. What if some members never contribute or seem hostile about participating?

In some cases, Data Teams have been imposed on school faculties without proper up-front training or without proper support once implementation begins. As a result, some teachers may seem hostile or, at the very least, reluctant to participate.

A principal or building leadership team can introduce the Data Teams concept to the entire faculty at once, perhaps at a faculty meeting, to make expectations for behavior clear from the start. Some principals have modeled a Data Team meeting in a "fishbowl" or inner/outer circle fashion at a session like this in order to show teachers a team in action, observing the expected norms. Other principals have used video snippets of effective teams in action (like those available in The Center's Leadership and Learning Live DVD collection).

Of course, once meetings begin, if some team members do not fully engage, the first line of defense is the Data Team leader. The problem should be handled within the team if possible. If that doesn't work, an instructional coach, department chairperson, or assistant principal may be able to attend subsequent meetings and help resolve the problem. If both of these steps don't result in an improvement in the team member's interaction, then the principal may want to join the meetings, at least until the situation improves. The principal may also want to take additional action, like having a private conversation with the person involved.

4. How should we handle a member who doesn't get his work scored prior to the meeting?

It is not the responsibility of the Data Team leader or any other member of the team to "pick up the slack" for a team member who does not arrive at each meeting with scored work in hand, already sorted into proficient, nonproficient, or other performance categories as previously determined by the team.

That being said, it certainly does hinder the progress of the team if a member comes to a meeting with incomplete or missing data. *The meeting should still go on, however.* In the meeting minutes or notes, the recorder should just note for that particular teacher, "no data reported." A principal or other administrator who is actively monitoring Data Team minutes is ultimately responsible for dealing with the teacher who is noncompliant.

On the Data Team of which I was a member, a certain teacher often gave excuses about why he couldn't get his work scored in time for the meeting. Eventually, two other teachers on the team started scoring his work for him. So, what ensued? Did he suddenly learn responsibility and begin scoring his own work? No. He learned that others would do it for him. Sadly, by not scoring his own work as frequently as he should have, he missed out on a great deal of formative information that he could have used to adjust instruction, even before a Data Team meeting had occurred. And, sadly, he also learned that he did not need to be an engaged participant in the Data Teams process.

Questions about Instructional Strategies

1. What is a "common" strategy?

A common strategy is an instructional strategy that is employed by all members of the team. Ideally it is research based and not something the team has already used to address the learning problem that they have agreed to tackle. It is important for teams to consider strategies that are both research based and innovative when they select strategies for common use.

Many teams begin the Data Teams process by simply sorting student results into two categories: proficient (meeting standard) and nonproficient. While this is not a satisfactory level of delineating student performance, it is an acceptable beginning step. Later, teams need to differentiate work that is close to proficiency from work that is further away and also focus on those students who will most likely need extensive support or intervention to meet the standard.

At any level of sophistication of the Data Teams process, determining at least one common instructional strategy to implement in whole-class instruction is a worthy endeavor. This is the one strategy that will be used by all teachers on the team in the instructional cycle between the pre- and post-assessments so that the largest number of students possible meet the level of proficiency that has been established by the team.

Different strategies may also be determined for different groups of students, again based on what the students demonstrate about their learning on the common formative assessments. For students who are already proficient or above on a pre-assessment, for example, compacted curriculum, inquiry projects, or individual contracts may be desirable, and these are not strategies the team would select to enact in whole-class fashion. For students who are still in need of intensive intervention after a post-assessment, various strategies might be employed in both whole-class, small-group, and out-of-class situations. It's best if the team reserves ample time in their meetings to discuss all the possible uses of instructional strategies—for the entire team, groups of students, and individuals.

2. Why are common strategies powerful?

One intent of the Data Teams process is to move the masses so that overall school improvement is impacted like never before; this is the essence of large-scale reform. The masses can be moved best by several adults putting their heads together and enacting innovative instructional practices together. This is a core supposition of the concept of the Professional Learning Communities model proposed by Richard and Rebecca DuFour and also by Mike Schmoker in his series of *Results* books. In addition to "in the moment" strategies individual teachers might employ in their classrooms in response to student needs, common strategies are essential for rapid, dramatic improvement and for replication that leads to ongoing improvement.

3. What if team members aren't well informed about research-based strategies?

Sometimes Data Team members are not well informed about best practices. Instructional coaches and others in the school building who study and utilize research-based strategies can be excellent resources for Data Teams. They can participate in meetings, model strategies during meetings or in teachers' classes, refer team members to helpful resources, and meet one-on-one with teachers to discuss changes in instructional practice.

Many building principals also devote ample time to the professional development of their teachers when Data Teams are implemented. Thus, staff meetings are often replaced with true professional learning sessions.

Some faculties engage in book studies to become better informed about research-based strategies. Several books that have proved popular with The Center's clients in the past few years include *Classroom Instruction That Works* (Marzano, Pickering, and Pollock, 2004), *The Art and Science of Teaching* (Marzano, 2007), and *Visible Learning: A Synthesis of Over 800 Meta-Analyses Relating to Achievement* (Hattie, 2008).

4. What resources are available to help teachers determine strategies?

Several resources have been very useful to our clients over the years. The books mentioned in the previous answer have been used widely.

More recently, The Center has developed a two-day seminar and training manual called *Power Strategies for Effective Teaching*. This material synthesizes the research and recommendations in over 50 other works. In 2008, the book *Visible Learning: A Synthesis of Over 800 Meta-Analyses Relating to Achievement* (Hattie, 2008) was published. This powerful work is currently being studied by Center associates so that it can be better reflected in seminars and support visits to sites using Data Teams.

Questions about Assessments

1. What kinds of assessments should Data Teams use?

Data Teams use short-cycle, brief assessments, generally called common formative assessments (CFAs). By short-cycle, we at The Center mean that each assessment covers a month or less of course material. Remember that the most effective Data Teams meet at least every other week. These teams often have assessments that cover only a few days' worth of material. They are assessing and responding to student needs continuously, and this kind of responsive teaching requires frequent, short assessments.

By brief, we mean that the assessment should not take most students more than one class period to complete. In the elementary grades, teachers must use their best judgment, but many elementary CFAs last no more than 30 minutes.

These assessments are not nearly as lengthy as standardized tests. They are tightly focused on the most important learning targets in the current "chunk" of learning.

In some cases, especially for assessments of writing, a Data Teams assessment may take longer than 30 minutes for students to complete. However, a rule of thumb, especially for secondary classes, is that a Data Teams assessment should not take more than one class period.

2. When are the assessments created?

Data Teams do not have time to create the assessments during meetings in which they are working through the five basic meeting steps. Therefore, the assessments must be created at other times—during common planning times, on in-service or early-release days, during summer curriculum work times, and so on.

Ideally, in the year before Data Teams are implemented, there is summer curriculum work that includes the development of these short-cycle assessments. If it is not possible to orchestrate summer curriculum work, then at the very least, the first few formative assessments to be used by Data Teams need to be completed before school actually begins, perhaps during the teacher workdays that precede the arrival of students.

If Data Teams can schedule times to meet every week, it is conceivable that the development of common assessments would occur at meetings at which no fresh data is available.

3. What if the assessments used, upon reflection, were not as good as they could have been? What should a team do in this case?

The team should still analyze the student work and the data that resulted. Of course any given assessment might not yield the information that was initially sought, but the student work can nonetheless yield important insights about what students know and can do.

Don't allow your team to avoid addressing student learning needs because the assessment isn't perfect. Once this kind of excuse is used, a detrimental precedent has been established. Teachers can learn something about student learning from any assessment task. A Data Team must seek information regardless of the quality of the assessment—in this case, because it has already been administered. Surely it wasn't a total waste of students' time and something can be learned.

Appendix

Instructional Data Team Meeting Rubric

Step	Proficient	Exemplary All Proficient Criteria PLUS:	Comments
Step 1: Collect and chart data	a) Data is assembled in discussion format prior to start of meeting	a) Results are disaggregated according to specific subgroups present in the school	
	b) Results include number, percentage, and names of students at multiple performance levels (e.g., Goal, Proficient, Close to Proficient, Intervention)	b) All team members, including support personnel who may not be able to attend meeting, have results	
	c) Data is disaggregated by grade-level standard if multiple standards are included on the assessment in order to support specific analysis	c) Data is triangulated (multiple sources of data are included that further illuminate students' knowledge and skill in the area being examined)	
	d) Data is disaggregated by teacher		
	e) Data supports timely, specific, and relevant feedback to teachers and students to improve performance		
	f) Data includes student work samples from the assessment being reviewed		
Step 2: Analyze data and prioritize needs	a) The inferring of strengths and needs is based on a direct analysis of student work	a) Prioritized needs reflect areas that will have impact within multiple skill areas	
	b) Analysis includes comparison of student work samples to targeted "unwrapped" standards	b) Needs inferred for intervention group are categorized according to a hierarchy of prerequisite skills	
	c) Strengths and needs identified are within the direct influence of teachers		

Step	Proficient	Exemplary All Proficient Criteria PLUS:	Comments
Step 2: Analyze data and prioritize needs	d) Team goes beyond labeling the need, or the "what," to infer the root cause, or the "why"		
	e) Strengths and needs are identified for each "performance group" (i.e., "Close to proficient" students, "Far to Go but Likely to achieve proficiency" students, etc.)		
	f) Needs are prioritized to reflect those areas that will have the largest impact within subject areas (if three or more needs are identified; otherwise prioritization may be implied)		
Step 3: Establish SMART goals	a) Establish, review, or revise a goal	a) Targeted needs have impact in multiple skill areas, e.g., "identifying supporting details"	
	b) **S**pecific targeted subject area, grade level, and student group are established	b) Intervention students have a goal related to prerequisite skills necessary for proficiency	
	c) **M**easurable area of need is established and assessment to be used is identified		
	d) **A**chievable gains in student learning are determined based on the consideration of current performance of all students		
	e) **R**elevant goal addresses needs of students and supports School Improvement Plan		
	f) **T**ime frame established for learning to occur, and for the subsequent administration of the assessment		

Step	Proficient	Exemplary All Proficient Criteria PLUS:	Comments
Step 4: Select instructional strategies	a) Strategies directly target the prioritized needs identified during the analysis	a) Strategies selected impact multiple skill areas	
	b) Strategies chosen will modify teachers' instructional practice	b) Modeling of how selected strategies would be implemented occurs during the meeting	
	c) Strategies describe actions of adults that change the thinking of students	c) Team members anticipate/discuss acceptable, ongoing adaptations to strategy implementation—"If... then..." *(There is a strong connection here to results indicators)*	
	d) Team describes strategies for each performance group	d) Team evaluates its capacity to use the selected instructional strategy and identifies needed resources, etc.	
	e) Team agrees on prioritized research-based strategies that will have greatest impact		
	f) Descriptions of strategies are specific enough to allow for replication (i.e., implementation, frequency, duration, resources)		
Step 5: Determine results indicators	a) Results indicators are created for each selected strategy	a) Team establishes interim time frame to monitor the implementation of the strategy	
	b) Indicators describe what the teacher will be doing if the strategy is being implemented	b) Indicators contain clear and detailed descriptions that allow others to replicate the described practices	
	c) Indicators describe what the students will be doing if the strategy is being implemented	c) Indicators are specific enough to allow teachers to predict student performance on next assessment	

Step	Proficient	Exemplary All Proficient Criteria PLUS:	Comments
Step 5: Determine results indicators	d) Indicators describe the anticipated change in student performance if the strategy is having the desired impact on the prioritized need		
Step 6: Monitor and evaluate results	a) Teachers bring student work samples that provide evidence of strategy implementation	a) Multiple work samples are included that show the progression of strategy implementation over time	
	b) Teachers describe their implementation of the strategy including frequency, direct instruction/modeling, and feedback provided to students	b) Teachers observe colleagues in their use of the strategy and discuss observations during this meeting	
	c) Teachers examine the student work samples to determine the quality of strategy implementation	c) Teachers discuss other situations where the strategy may be used	
	d) Teachers examine the work samples to determine whether the strategy is having the desired impact (effectiveness)		
	e) Teachers support each other in the use of the strategy through specific dialog, modeling, planning, etc.		
	f) Teachers discuss the effectiveness of the strategy including whether to continue, modify, or stop the use of the selected strategy		

Step	Proficient	Exemplary All Proficient Criteria PLUS:	Comments
Norms and participation	a) Team members actively listen (delay response, rephrase statements, clarify)	a) Agreed-upon norms are internalized (requiring no reminders or references)	
	b) Team members assume the positive intentions of others (respond as if all members are well intentioned)	b) Team serves as a model for professional behavior	
	c) Team operates by developed norms	c) Members apply learned practices to classrooms and serve as models for other team members or teachers	
	d) Members openly reflect on own instructional practices	d) Members actively solicit ideas, successes, and challenges from each other	
	e) Members share ideas, successes, and challenges	e) Members assist other team members in adhering to stated time frames and purpose of meeting	
	f) Members adhere to meeting time and purpose		
	g) Members bring student evidence and other required resources to meeting		
	h) Members review norms before each meeting (i.e., verbally, on minutes, posted, etc.)		
	i) Members reflect on their adherence to the norms at the end of the meeting and identify next steps if needed		

Step	Proficient	Exemplary All Proficient Criteria PLUS:	Comments
Agenda	a) Follows the steps of the Data Teams process	a) Includes reminders of agreed-upon norms	
	b) Indicates targeted instructional area and standards	b) Includes reminders and descriptions of roles	
	c) Includes next meeting date	c) Includes reflections of current team status against goal as appropriate (results from previous assessment, pre-assessment, etc.)	
	d) Allocates time for each component of meeting		
	e) Focused entirely on collaborative analysis of student work		
	f) Includes items related to next steps		
Minutes	a) Accurate representation of meeting process	a) Available at the end of the meeting	
	b) Includes list of members present	b) Record of collaboration, analysis, and strategies that allows for replication of practices by professionals outside of the team	
	c) Indicates prioritized needs for team focus	c) Minutes include models for strategy use	
	d) Describes agreed-upon strategies	d) Minutes include list of supporting resources (Web sites, etc.)	
	e) Descriptions of results indicators reflect desired changes in student and teacher behaviors		
	f) Descriptions of strategies are specific and allow team members to implement with consistency agreed-upon actions		
	g) Descriptions of results indicators are specific and allow team members to implement with consistency agreed-upon actions		

Step	Proficient	**Exemplary** All Proficient Criteria PLUS:	Comments
Minutes	h) Available within 24 hours		
	i) Descriptive enough for leadership to be able to identify team needs and required supports		
	j) Minutes are taken during the meeting in order to capture group thinking (not re-created after the meeting)		
Schedule	a) Meetings are held weekly for a minimum of 45 minutes	a) Meetings are held within two days of the availability of the data	
	b) Monitoring meetings are scheduled to collaborate on strategy implementation and make required adjustments (formal or informal)	b) Resource personnel scheduled to support EACH meeting	
	c) Meetings are held within one week of availability of data		
	d) Meeting time is uninterrupted		
	e) Appropriate resource personnel are scheduled to meet with teams on a regular basis		
Administration	a) Delineates clear timelines and responsibilities for resources/supports identified during Data Team meeting	a) Provides support to team immediately	
	b) Provides support to team within identified timelines	b) Serves as a model for administrative support of Data Teams process	
	c) Plans for necessary supports during the school-wide Data Team meeting	c) Provides regular opportunities for team members to publicly share their successes during faculty meetings or through other means	
	d) Is knowledgeable, supportive, and respectful of the Data Teams process	d) Provides structures that allow teacher modeling and observation of successful practices	

Step	Proficient	Exemplary All Proficient Criteria PLUS:	Comments
Administration	e) Promptly provides support that develops the team's proficiency in the Data Teams process	e) Is present during meeting and leaves with clearly identified action steps to support team's decisions	
	f) Models an inquiry-based approach (defined as facilitating the action research-based learning of the faculty and linking student achievement results to adult variables rather than mandating specific practices)		
	g) Is aware of team goals and identified, prioritized areas of need		
	h) Is aware of instructional practices selected and provides feedback on the appropriateness of the strategies		
	i) Is knowledgeable about effective teaching strategies and provides the coaching and feedback necessary for successful implementation		
	j) Attends at least one Data Team meeting per month		

References

Allen, J. (1999). *Words, words, words: Teaching vocabulary in grades 4–12.* York, ME: Stenhouse.

Anderson, K. R. (2010). *Data teams success stories, volume 1.* Englewood, CO: Lead + Learn Press.

Brandt, R. (2003, Winter). Is this school a learning organization? 10 ways to tell. *Journal of Staff Development, 24*(1), 10–16.

DuFour, R. (2010, October 27). Why educators should be given time to collaborate. *Education Week, 30*(9), 15.

DuFour, R., DuFour, R., Eaker, R., & Many, T. (2006). *Learning by doing: A handbook for professional learning communities at work.* Bloomington, IN: Solution Tree Press.

Duke, D. (2007). Turning schools around: What we are learning about the process, and those who do it. *Education Week, 26*(24), 35–37.

Garmston, R., & Wellman, B. (2002). *The adaptive school: A sourcebook for developing collaborative groups: Syllabus.* 4th ed. Norwood, MA: Christopher-Gordon Publishers.

Graves, M. (2005). *The vocabulary book: Learning and instruction.* Urbana, IL: National Council of Teachers of English.

Leadership and Learning Center, The. (2006a). *Common formative assessments seminar.*

Leadership and Learning Center, The. (2006b). *Data teams seminar.* 2nd ed.

Leadership and Learning Center, The. (2009). *Power strategies for effective teaching seminar.*

Leadership and Learning Center, The. (2010). *Data teams seminar.* 3rd ed.

Marzano, R. J. (2004). *Building background knowledge for academic achievement: Research on what works in schools.* Alexandria, VA: Association for Curriculum and Staff Development.

Reeves, D. B. (2002). *The leader's guide to standards: A blueprint for educational equity and excellence.* New York: Jossey-Bass.

Reeves, D. B. (2008). *Reframing teacher leadership to improve your school.* Alexandria, VA: Association for Curriculum and Staff Development.

Reeves, D. B. (2009). *Leading change in your school: How to conquer myths, build commitment, and get results.* Alexandria, VA: Association for Curriculum and Staff Development.

Reeves, D. B. (2010). *Finding your leadership focus: What matters most for student results.* New York: Teachers College Press.

Schmoker, M. J. (2004). Tipping point: From feckless reform to substantive instructional improvement. *Phi Delta Kappan, 85*(6), 424–432.

Schmoker, M. J. (2006). *Results now: How we can achieve unprecedented improvements in teaching and learning.* Alexandria, VA: Association for Curriculum and Staff Development.

White, S. H. (2005). *Beyond the numbers: Making data work for teachers and school leaders.* Englewood, CO: Lead + Learn Press.

Index